THE PERFECT MIX

THE
PERFECT
MIX

Everything I Know About
Leadership I Learned
as a Bartender

Helen Rothberg, PhD

ATRIA BOOKS

New York   London   Toronto   Sydney   New Delhi

ATRIA
BOOKS

An Imprint of Simon & Schuster, Inc.
1230 Avenue of the Americas
New York, NY 10020

First Atria Books hardcover edition June 2017

ATRIA BOOKS and colophon are trademarks of Simon & Schuster, Inc.

For information about special discounts for bulk purchases, please contact Simon & Schuster Special Sales at 1-866-506-1949 or business@simonandschuster.com.

The Simon & Schuster Speakers Bureau can bring authors to your live event. For more information or to book an event, contact the Simon & Schuster Speakers Bureau at 1-866-248-3049 or visit our website at www.simonspeakers.com.

Interior design by Amy Trombat

Manufactured in the United States of America

10 9 8 7 6 5 4 3 2 1

Library of Congress Cataloging-in-Publication Data is available.

ISBN 978-1-5011-2782-3
ISBN 978-1-5011-2784-7 (ebook)

Certain names and other characteristics have been changed. In addition, some people portrayed are composites.

Thanks, Dad

CONTENTS

THE PERFECT MIX

Introduction

AS AN EDUCATOR AND consultant, I have been training leaders and future leaders for more than twenty-five years. I have worked with undergraduate business majors and MBAs as well as with executives of Fortune 500 firms and not-for-profits, government officials, and entrepreneurs in technology start-ups. Over that quarter century I have worked in organizational change, helping people accept that something in their work lives will be different; strategic planning, helping organizations choose a course for the future; and competitive intelligence, the very deliberate gathering of actionable information about industries and competitors. This is not spying but sleuthing. Not Dumpster diving or bugging boardrooms. Instead, I engage in detective work: investigating, discovering, integrating, and analyzing information from people and published sources about companies and the business environment. Competitive intelligence facilitates strategic planning, which itself may be an impetus for organizational change.

Through all these pursuits I came to realize that, even more than from academic credentials or experience, everything I know about management and leadership—everything essential I know about becoming successful—I learned as a bartender.

I was in the garden section of Lowe's on a warm July afternoon, considering how big a pot I needed to replant my ficus trees, when my phone buzzed. I accepted the call, and before I could even say hello, I heard, "Dr. Rothberg, can you talk?" It was Gabe Gambino, a recent graduate with a BS in business. No matter how many times I told him that he could call me Helen, the familiar title stuck.

Gabe and his crew of friends had planned and prodded their way into and through my strategic-management class. They had taken full advantage of my office hours, scheduling weekly meetings for themselves and their teams working on projects. If they saw my door open or the light on, they'd come in for encouragement, counseling, and chocolates. One month before his capstone analysis—a thorough, real-time strategic plan for a publicly traded company—was due, a distressed Gabe sat in my office and admitted that he didn't think he could complete it. He had waited too long to begin—he actually had not yet started writing at all—and the job felt too big. I knew from experience that half of his anxiety would be relieved just by starting and I put him on the "Aunt Helen Plan": He had to e-mail me every evening and tell me exactly what he had accomplished that day. When I didn't hear from him by 10:30 one night, I e-mailed him: "Where's Gabe?"

Gabe's final plan was excellent and after graduation he'd gotten a corporate sales job where he thought he was joining a full-service advertising agency with established clients. The reality was that he had to hunt for clients to represent, but the clients he could approach didn't have resources to even consider buying what he was selling. Ergo, his call to me.

"Dr. Rothberg, I hate my job," Gabe said, and, without taking a single breath, went on to tell me that he got up every morning at 5:00 a.m. to catch the train, sat at a desk all day cold-calling, and worked on commission. "I'm losing money going to work, I get rejected all day, I don't relate to the people in my office. I don't see this leading to anything. This isn't what I went to college for. I'm not good at this. I am miserable."

"Quit the job, Gabe," I said as I put down the pot I'd been considering and walked to another aisle.

"I can't quit my job. I am the first in my family to graduate from college. I have bills to pay. What am I going to do? I don't want to get up in the morning anymore."

"Quit the job, Gabe."

"I can't."

I understood how Gabe felt. I remembered my first real job, waitressing at a Catskills deli/American-Chinese restaurant. The most senior waitress, a lifer, got all the best tables: couples who had cocktails with dinner. As the youngest, I got the worst tables: multigenerational families who could never order everything they wanted at the same time. One evening the lifer dropped mashed potatoes outside the kitchen door and left them without a warning. I came barreling through with a full tray, slipping and falling on my butt in front of my table of eight, who watched their food land on me and everywhere else but in front of their hungry selves. The week before that, an angry chef chased me with his meat cleaver because I wouldn't bring him a whiskey sour during the dinner service. I hated the place but was afraid to quit. No one wanted to hire "a kid." I needed the experience and I needed the money. But the potatoes in my braids were the last straw.

Not every job is a good job. After I quit, I was able to find a better restaurant where there were tablecloths, nicer chefs, and better tips. A few years later, when I realized that waitresses' tips reflect many things outside of their control—how quickly the kitchen gets the meal ready, how good the food is, how many times a water glass is filled—I moved to bartending, where there was a more direct link between my effort and reward. This was a better fit for me. And because of that I blossomed.

It took forty-five minutes of coaxing and searching three aisles of flowerpots, but Gabe agreed to quit his job and I found the right pot. Within two months he began a new career as a sales coordinator and moved out of his parents' home to his own place in Brooklyn. Within two and a half years he was promoted to account executive.

You have to close one door for another to open. You have to let go of the sure thing—the bird in the hand or the flowerpot or the job—in order to be able to take hold of what you want and to find a place where you can shine. You have to find your fit.

Sometimes people stay in positions because it's what they know and they think it's what is expected of them: they think they have to "tough it out," they don't want to let people down, or they're afraid there is nothing else. They start losing faith in what they bring to the table. They get lost.

Companies do this as well. One of my first consulting clients was the Solgar vitamin company. A leader in the early eighties health food industry, Solgar had only seven or eight sales representatives to service more than two thousand accounts across fifty states. We had challenging conversations about the value of all those accounts. It was their belief that every customer was a good customer. My contention was that not all customers have equal appeal. Some ordered so little, paid their accounts so late, and required so much attention from the sales force that the company was actually losing money servicing them.

This was a very hard reality for Solgar to accept. They had built their business years ago by visiting every small health food store in New York. It was in their DNA to treat all accounts the same. They kept trying to run the company as if their sales were to only a handful of buyers. They were stuck. Their business model no longer fit who they had become.

After a change in leadership, a compromise was reached. While all accounts remained in the portfolio, not all were serviced the same way. Most were open to new ways of learning about new products. The accounts that didn't like the change complained, but they still carried Solgar because their customers wanted their products. With new marketing materials and a focused sales force, Solgar's sales and profit margins flourished.

When I shifted from waitressing to bartending, my receipts grew as well. In both positions I needed to be attentive and respectful to each customer. Regardless of whatever attitudes customers brought to the table or bar, I was courteous. However, as a waitress I had less control of all the moving parts, so I held back my personality some. Disgruntled diners don't often appreciate a humorous and cheeky waitress, and I would have to gracefully shoulder customer dissatisfaction that I wasn't responsible for. As a bartender, I didn't have to hold back. I not only had more control over what I mixed and delivered but I also was able—like Solgar's sales force, like Gabe—to customize my service and work from my strengths.

Creating a good fit—for yourself and your company—matters. Sometimes you have to be willing to take the leap, to trust that you have the right ingredients to bring the best of yourself—and the best of your company—to the right situation. A good fit can be the difference between surviving and thriving, between being busy and working well, between working hard and working smart. Sometimes you need to give yourself permission to discover what else is possible. People, situations, commerce, emotions, workers, bosses, customers, food, alcohol—these can be either a combustible or harmonizing blend. Learning how to read a situation and be deliberate in how I managed and responded— which parts of my personality to shine or quiet—helped me create a fit with my surroundings. Getting involved with bartending, mingling management and cocktails, brought me to a place where I could learn what works and what doesn't, what mixes well and what should never be combined. It was the foundation for all that came later.

———

There are many recipes for leadership; the one I have come to after all these years is **ADVICE**:

Action
Determination
Vision
Integrity
Communication
Empathy

And with each ingredient—Action, Determination, Vision, Integrity, Communication, and Empathy—leaders know who they are and who they may need to become. They recognize that life is fluid and what has worked in the past might not work in the future. They are confident seekers of knowledge. They embrace what is new and unknown with courage and grace.

What does this have to do with bartending? Everything. It includes being astute, giving people what they want, and keeping things running smoothly. It also includes managing infuriating, delightful, and sometimes dangerous clients, as well as temperamental and talented employees and even owners with brilliant ideas who don't communicate well but are surprisingly wise. In doing all this, you find strength in yourself that you didn't know was there.

This is life behind the bar. This is life leading an organization. Sometimes you stir, sometimes you shake, and sometimes you blend. And sometimes you just serve it up neat, just as it is. Bartenders develop the instinct to know what to do and when to stand back and watch, when to share what they know and when to say nothing. That is why they give great ADVICE. That is why bartending is a model for leadership.

This book is populated by situations and characters based on real events and people (with some of their names and other details changed) and some who are composites. It serves up what I've learned from my experiences working with an amalgam of characters in different situations at the bar. Uncannily, they mirror what I lived professionally with teams at big companies like Kellogg, technology start-ups like Concept Five Technologies, and not-for-profits like Good Reasons. The lessons I learned have worked in industries as varied as advertising, education, energy, and medical technology. I share these stories, pairing them with their bar-mates, inspiring a nugget of wisdom and a unique component of the leadership cocktail. And, of course, there are cocktails, too. The drink recipes are my own.

I invite you to share my experiences, enjoy a drink, and sip some ADVICE. I hope you discover that a well-balanced concoction of people, choices, situations, and lessons is possible in your own career and that it can be enjoyable, informative, and satisfying.

ADVICE FOR LEADERSHIP

1

ACTION: Outside Insights

SPRINGTIME ON EAST TWENTY-SIXTH Street and Park Avenue South bloomed with possibility. I was approaching my first summer break en route to an MBA from the City University of New York's graduate business program at Baruch College. I needed to find the right bartending job to sustain me.

I had outlined my priorities on a spreadsheet:

- A twenty-minute walk from school to give me time to switch gears.
- Ample public and taxi transportation for convenience and safety.
- A lively neighborhood, also for safety. I had worked downtown, where office buildings emptied at 6:00 p.m., leaving either desolate sidewalks or late-night partiers stumbling into dance halls.
- A smallish place that also served food. I didn't want to have to strain to hear over music with a throbbing bass and push drinks to nameless people.

Heading east along Twenty-Sixth Street, I rejected Lexington Avenue because it was too residential, continued to Third Avenue, and turned south.

Third Avenue was close enough to school to be convenient but far enough away to be anonymous, where professors were not likely to go. The Gramercy Park neighborhood was swank, with an upscale mix of businesses and apartment buildings. The streets hummed with people ready to drink, eat, and spend money day and night. Yellow cabs cruised around the clock. Pizza shops, Chinese takeout, an Italian deli, a liquor store, three boutiques, and four Irish pubs lined the four-block walk to Twenty-Second Street. While the pubs had interchangeable menus and prices, they differed in their advertised entertainment. Any bar with karaoke and happy-hour all-you-can-eat chicken wings and dollar pints was off the list—too much noise for too little money.

Duffy's on Twenty-First Street had a specials board and live acoustic music on Thursday nights, so I went in to feel the place out. With a sawdust floor, wooden tables, and a small platform stage, Duffy's was dark, smoky, and boisterous. I sat at the corner of the bar closest to the window, where I could see the layout and watch how things ran. I had a spreadsheet with me and was ready to fill it with notes. A red-faced round man wearing a folded-over apron served me a glass of house wine with a bowl of peanuts, then quickly returned to the gaggle of guys perched in front of the beer taps.

The place reminded me of my first bartending experience at the Gable Inn, a small neighborhood bar in Bayside, Queens, with a lively blue-collar crowd. That's where I first met Pat, a woman who would have a big impact on my life.

Working as a bartender, Pat was a mentor, Yoda, teacher, and friend. With her thick black eyelashes, blue eye shadow, and blond pixie helmet hair, Pat managed the needs of a six-person waitstaff and scores of patrons with a gentility and steadfast calm I had yet to see in anyone else. She could shut down a sassy waitress with a look, have patrons wait ten minutes for drinks without complaining, and somehow keep the moody hostess smiling.

I wanted to be like Pat, so I started going in early to help her set up and learn from her. She would give me advice on handling the grouchy cook, my mother, school, boys, or anything that was troubling me. She taught me how to make Bloody Mary mix, cut lime twists, and rim a glass with salt. She shared her work philosophies, which I realized later were actually life philosophies. Pat taught me how to manage and take control, how to become a bartender.

––––––

By 5:00 p.m. it was happy hour at Duffy's, and an after-work crowd who drank mostly tap beer while eating mozzarella sticks and clams on the half shell started filtering in. The waiters came and went from behind the bar to grab bottles of beer, run the soda tap, and drop their drink orders. Back at the Gable Inn, Pat never let anyone behind her bar: "My money drawer, my responsibility." She ran progress tapes for the manager to check, had the barback leave cases of beer and clean glasses on the service end, and restocked herself. Pat had a system for setting up her bar. Bottles needed for making the most popular drinks were the easiest to reach. Spotless glasses were positioned strategically so that the waitresses could set them up with their orders on trays. The tools of her trade—paring knife, cigarette lighter, and corkscrew—were never left out of their drawer. Pat's bar had a high shine, and she had everything under control. But that was not how Duffy's was managed. I noted all this on my spreadsheet. Duffy's seemed like a busy place, but I was looking for something different: a place where imported beer, cocktails, and something other than bar pies and burgers was served. I left and kept walking south.

Between Nineteenth and Twentieth Streets, tucked among buildings tall and small, was a three-story redbrick building with white window trims and a dark plate-glass window with "Cincinnati" painted in pink lettering. I looked in. A small restaurant seating fifty-four, it had a beautiful oak bar opposite four tall banquets. I walked around the block to check out the neighborhood. On one corner was the New York City Police Academy. I liked that. The boys in blue would be a welcome sight at closing time around 3:00 a.m. Around the other was Cabrini Medical Center. Hospital folk drink when they get off duty. In a four-block radius none of the other bars or restaurants was as well situated or as elegant, or had as pricey a menu. It felt perfect.

The next day at 4:00 p.m., the quiet time before the dinner crowd arrived, I perched at the far end of the bar. A tall, brown-haired guy in a tan oxford shirt and blue jeans poured me a glass of white wine. A few people were nursing drinks, reading the paper, and eating peanuts. At 4:30 my glass was empty. Even though the bar was not busy, the bartender never came back to offer me a refill. This was a nicer bar than Duffy's, but it wasn't as busy and the service wasn't great. I sensed the opportunity to build here. I finally caught the bartender's attention and inquired whether there was a position open. He went upstairs to get the owner. An hour later Andrew came down to meet me.

Handsome and strongly built, Andrew was in his late twenties. He knew that he was handsome and strongly built. We shook hands and sized each other up. He liked that I went to school and lived nearby, that I had experience, that I wasn't an actor. Actors in New York also fill roles in many restaurants. We agreed that I would shadow a couple of shifts before getting a slot in the schedule. He called Marco over from the dining room to set it up.

"Who's Marco?" I was confused.

"He's our headwaiter. Might as well shadow the best to learn how we do it."

"Why would I shadow a waiter? I'm applying for a bartender position," I said. Andrew squared his shoulders and said, "I don't hire women bartenders."

I thought he was kidding. This was 1982, not 1952. But he wasn't kidding. Andrew didn't think that women were strong enough to lift cases of beer or tough enough to cut people off and get them to leave. I was stubborn and didn't like being told no. I wasn't letting go. Cincinnati was my perfect place. I had to do something fast.

I offered him a deal: I'd work the busiest night behind the bar for free. No shadowing. No bullshit. "The only thing you have at risk is being wrong." It was a hard offer to refuse, and he didn't.

As I walked toward home down Third Avenue, the adrenaline from my win was overcome by dread. What had I just gotten myself into? I had never worked a place like Cincinnati before. It was elegant and had a sophisticated menu. In the hour and a half I had sat at the bar watching the place and the people, I had realized that the Gramercy Park crowd was a different breed of clientele and waitstaff. I had always been a downtown, working-class girl and felt most comfortable in a melting pot of color, spices, and accents. These customers were uptown and drank things I had never heard of: Lillet, Pernod, Chambord. They ate food you'd find in beach surf—oysters, escargot, and crab—and traveled on the weekends to elite society places like the Hamptons, Nantucket, Mantoloking. A species all their own. Dangerous, intimidating, unknowable. Better. And better made me fear that I wouldn't be sophisticated enough, smart enough, or good enough. But the waitstaff was eccentric. Actors, singers, and dancers juggling shifts and showcases at small, tucked-away clubs, changing their names and memorizing menus, they were big personalities used to getting rejected and expecting to be pampered for it.

And yet I still wagered: "I'll work for free and then you can decide." This was early muscle memory. In my experience, survival came more from deliberate, careful action than from words.

ADVICE: Do more, say less.

Fear was not an option for me growing up on Grand Street on the Lower East Side. Fear has its own color and smell, and those enticed by it could pick up its sweet scent from two blocks away. Fear made you gather information before taking any action. You made your every step cautious and deliberate, because if you didn't, you got your ass kicked. Knowing which streets to walk down, where to shoot hoops, who to let buy you a soda, was intelligence. You shared it with your inner circle. Craftiness, or in some cases brashness, was the perfume I needed to mask the fear. When scared, I was tough and resourceful. This worked more times than not, and I learned it young. My slight build and scared self wanted to walk the streets or ride my bike with only one eye behind my back, not two. I didn't have an older brother around to watch out for me. I needed to build a reputation.

Outside PS 110, an elementary school on Delancey Street, I tried to push my way into pickup games of basketball and play with boys who were older, taller, and heavier than I was. I showed up every day after school and waited to be selected by a team, but I was ignored. After two weeks it was time to do something or give it up. I pulled the *You're afraid I'll make you sissies look stupid* card. The two captains flicked their hands toward me as if they were swatting a fly. I locked eyes with the big Italian boy with the dimple, Danny Alaimo.

"Okay, rookie, you play with my team, and after we wipe the courts with you, you can go home and play some girl games and leave us alone," they said, laughing at me now. In my head I said, *Screw you.* On the court, I took my position.

I tightened the laces of my pink high-tops and drove down the lane, ducking and throwing elbows, proving I had guts, that I was a little wild. I was knocked down, skinned my knees. I got elbowed, which blackened my eye, bloodied my nose, and busted my lip. I continued to play. I never called foul, whined, or cried. That day I earned a protector, Danny, and was referred to from then on as either "She crazy" or "Rookie."

On that basketball court, the code was to let your moves speak for you. Everyone talked shit. No one cared what you said, only what you did. I couldn't ask for protection. I had to earn it, without ever hinting that I wanted it. Show up, play hard, swallow the insults. Pay back by stealing the ball, making a free throw, and never answering my mother, Frieda, when she asked, "Tell me which of those boys threw their elbow in your face so I can mop the floor with him!" All that earned me the respect of Danny, who became my protector. But I had to show up and do, earn my own reputation, before I was able to get.

The dynamics of a basketball court are similar to those in an organization. The "team" is like a field of wildflowers: people with different backgrounds, from different cultures, and with different life experiences. A "win" can bring accolades or jealousy. A "rookie" has to walk the court carefully, watching, listening, and then proving herself with action, not words. Saying what you can do or sharing what you have done in a previous job means little. Getting things done with attention to detail—and on time—and showing what you are made of mean more than storytelling at lunchtime. Taking on a hard assignment is an opportunity to learn getting it right from getting it wrong.

My fear of the yuppie Gramercy Park breed was about not getting it right, about being too different from them. But the prospect of not stepping behind that bar, letting fear get the better of me, made me more anxious than the thought of doing so. It was time to lace up those high-tops again, be a rookie, and see what happened.

I showed up at Cincinnati on Friday at 4:00 p.m. My intention was to keep the dining room flowing and keep people lingering at the bar past 10:30 p.m. Andrew was looking for physical strength, but I knew he was looking at the wrong thing. I wanted to flex my management muscle. I was going to make his decision to hire me very easy. I tucked my *Mr. Boston Official Bartender's Guide* in the drawer near the service end with my corkscrew, cigarette lighter, and stash of pens. I introduced myself to the hostess, Liza, and the waiters and asked the staff what drinks were popular so I could reset the bar. I called over the *Don't you be asking me to do things* barback, Bruno, and gave him ten dollars as an advance toward his tip out. To ensure a steady flow of clean glasses, I had him fetch me a rack and give five dollars to the dishwasher. I had learned this from Pat: Figure out where the bottlenecks can be and incentivize the help you will need to manage them.

The dining room was busy that night, so people were eating appetizers at the bar while they waited for tables. The kitchen closed at 10:00, and the last patrons left the bar at 1:00 a.m. By 1:30, I'd restocked the bar for the next day and Andrew had his healthy register receipts. I'd proved myself and overcome my own fear.

Overcoming fear involves risk. My first night behind that bar, engaging with the patrons, I realized that most of what I feared was in my head. I had created a story based on my beliefs about the Gramercy Park crowd. Letting impressions and not actual experience create a story can distort reality and let you invent reasons why you shouldn't act, why you don't fit in, why anything you may think of doing will not make a difference. I thought that the uptown people were better because they were professionals, probably from Ivy League schools, living in expensive apartments, drinking expensive wine. I was a downtown city girl with a local education, more an example of survival of the fittest than of having been born with a silver spoon in my mouth. This didn't make the uptown folks better than I was, just different.

Pat showed me that while you can't always control the things you fear or the things that can happen to you, you can control how you respond. You can complain, whine, and make excuses or you can choose to do something. You can drive down the lane and throw your elbows. Sometimes when you throw elbows you get a black eye, but sometimes you also make the basket, and sometimes it is a little bit of both.

Leadership Is More Than Management

Management is about creating certainty in an uncertain world. Planning, organizing, communicating, and controlling are functions designed to create order, predictability, and outcomes. There is little room for risk taking. Leadership is about achieving vision. It is a gateway for risk taking.

Andrew took a risk. He went against his strongly held notion that men make better bartenders than women and gave me an opening to prove otherwise. He instinctively understood that my willingness to do more and say less, to show what I was capable of instead of arguing with his beliefs, gave him a window into who he would have working with him—if I was able to deliver. If I couldn't manage the bar, then he would be vindicated. If I could, he would get someone with initiative and more rounded skills than his current bartender. He realized that being wrong could be a good thing. With his current bartender, on busy nights, Andrew often would have to jump behind the bar and help. When drinks didn't make it to the waitstaff, then tables turned more slowly. He would work the service end, ring checks, and keep things moving. Andrew didn't have to do this during my trial shift.

He hired me, and I worked for him for five years. By taking action to put the right person in the right position, Andrew liberated his time to invest more effort on working *on* the business than *in* the business.

A leader's actions affect the well-being of many different stakeholders: employees, patrons, investors, and communities. Sometimes this responsibility creates a misguided sense that a leader always has to be right. Leaders are expected to be knowledgeable and experienced. That's why they are given authority and power and put in charge. We want them to be right because there is so much at stake. But no one is always right. Evolved leaders admit when they are wrong and then take action; they use the opportunity to learn and do things differently.

After the Bar

No Is Not an Option

Taking action doesn't mean jumping into something without thinking about it first, especially when your actions can affect others. That type of impulsiveness can create havoc. But so, too, can overthinking or overanalyzing a situation and not acting. Fear of the unknown, adverse outcomes, or personal disappointment can lead to inaction, which is when people, relationships, and organizations can get stuck.

When an organization has a quality issue, it needs to act: recall the product or suffer a damaged reputation, loss in market share, or a congressional investigation. Not dismissing an executive who harasses employees or other executives can result in hefty lawsuits. When a company's market share begins to shrink, not acting can mean losing a brand's leadership position and prime placement on the grocer's shelf.

When I taught at Rutgers University, I was lucky enough to have Benjamin Gilad take me under his wing. A former Israeli policeman, he was a professor of strategy and a founding member of the Strategic and Competitive Intelligence Professionals and the Academy of Competitive Intelligence, and he added competitive intelligence to my strategy and behavioral-science toolbox. When Kellogg hired him, he took me along to help.

At the time, Kellogg had had domestic supremacy in the breakfast cereal category for decades, but General Mills was closing the gap. Marketing had been king, using the Kellogg logo to push product off the grocery shelf, and so marketing managers were confident that spending more on marketing would close the gap. Gary E. Costly, then CEO, thought the loss of market share had more to do with General Mills' pricing strategy, and he knew it was time to go beyond marketing and to shake up the company. Having read *The Business Intelligence System: A New Tool for Competitive Advantage*, which Ben had coauthored, he decided to bring Ben to Kellogg to create a competitive analysis capability.

Ben hunted for intelligence acumen across the organization. In a small office in the back of the complex in Battle Creek, Michigan, Ben discovered a young geophysicist working as a food engineer. Jeff Webster had all the markings of a great intelligence officer. Unassuming, analytical, and courageous, Jeff was both smart and curious. He didn't say a lot, but when he did, he was insightful and on the mark. And he wasn't from Marketing. This was a potentially tough sell: to empower a person without the expected pedigree to have an impact on executive decision-making. Gary Costly took the risk. This was throwing elbows on the basketball court. Costly was preempting marketing by putting a food engineer in a strategic and community-relations role.

Jeff became the first competitive intelligence person at Kellogg with direct access to the CEO. His mission was to create a competitive and competitor landscape—in other words, to investigate, analyze, and craft a topography of the industry's dynamics and Kellogg's rivals' capabilities. He would be the one to provide the CEO with unfiltered and timely analysis, but in order to do so, he needed the support of the Kellogg knowledge community: people from across all departments—engineering, product development, supply-chain management, and human resources—who would share what they knew and help figure out what various bits of information really meant.

I was brought in to help Webster create "shadow" teams that would become experts on competitors. He gathered employees and managers from different departments and levels and invited them to a three-day off-site workshop where we gave them analytical tools. More important, we began to change the culture. Getting people to tell the truth about what worked and what didn't was harder than getting people to buy into the importance of sharing what they knew. For Jeff to be successful, he needed his network to give him unfiltered information, even if it was unsettling.

We trained the teams—one each to research General Mills, Post, and Quaker Oats, and two teams for Kellogg—and gave them their first assignment. They were to create profiles of the competitors they were assigned that identified those companies' future goals and assumptions about the industry, as well as their strengths, weaknesses, and strategies. They were given eight weeks to prepare a presentation for the executive suite. The teams were very nervous about delivering news to senior management that their own management was not vetting first.

Politically, this was never done. Executives never received unfiltered or candid reports from lower-level employees. Their managers framed information before it was shared upward.

However, employees on the shadow teams believed in the importance of reporting unfiltered information even if it was bad news. This is a pillar of the intelligence process. The teams studying Post, General Mills, and Quaker Oats got the intel on Kellogg's competitors; they discovered that the other companies were using the same engineering company to build their manufacturing equipment, erasing any design advantages Kellogg had had in the past. General Mills had a more efficient supply-chain management process and thus strong profit margins. Kellogg's rivals assumed that Kellogg was satisfied with its market position, which made Kellogg complacent and thus vulnerable to aggressive competitive action.

But when it came time to make their presentations to senior management, the shadow teams did not have the courage to do so. They omitted some key information from their presentations that Ben, Jeff, and I thought was crucial.

Ben and I coached Jeff that there was only one choice to make: to bring the complete Kellogg analysis straight to the CEO. He had to take action and prove that his new position was important to the well-being of the firm. Not doing so would render the work of the shadow teams an academic exercise and not the building blocks of an intelligence capability.

Jeff brought the Kellogg teams' findings and his analysis of the data to Costly. The CEO didn't like what he heard and didn't agree with Jeff's conclusions, but what he disliked even more was that this type of information and analysis had never reached his desk before—that his management team had always massaged and framed analyses to make them more palatable.

Costly was convinced from that day forward that the intelligence position was essential and that Jeff Webster, cereal scientist, was the right guy for the job. He took a risk and shook up his company by structuring an "Office of the President" with a direct line of communication to the CEO. Jeff Webster was to bring him daily news feeds and situational analyses that had input from Marketing but weren't controlled by Marketing. Today, Kellogg Company continues to outperform General Mills in return on assets (ROA), return on equity (ROE), and earnings per share (EPS).

———

Kellogg and Jeff Webster, and Cincinnati and I, had a lot in common. Both companies were facing situations that called for action: General Mills was gaining on Kellogg's market share, and Cincinnati's bar was not as busy as those of its competitors. Jeff and I also had to take action to prove that we belonged in the positions we were vying for. We each needed to have an early success so that "No" from management would not be an option. We both would become vital ingredients to the future business and catalysts for culture change, Jeff through competitive intelligence and me by making the bar a destination. We had to overcome fear. For Jeff it was breaking with the norm and giving his CEO unedited analysis. I had to overcome the fear that I wasn't good enough to work in an upscale bar.

Yet it was actually our outsider-ness that made us both so successful. We were able to break stereotypes and provide fresh perspectives on how things worked. Instead of paralyzing us with fear, our outsider status compelled us to take action, to face that which seemed most daunting. And what was daunting actually became heartening, as Jeff realized that the Office of the President was a real change, and I realized that there really wasn't that much difference between me and the uptown folks except money.

The Drink

THE GRAND STREET

3 ounces vodka
Splash of water
2 tablespoons Italian lemon ice
4 ripe blueberries

Blend the ingredients. Add a twist of risk and a dash of action. Pour over ice.

Taking action in the face of fear or uncertainty can create anxiety. It can require some shape-shifting: taking on new characteristics to step into something less familiar. Becoming an uptown bartender, or an intelligence analyst when you are a cereal scientist, is shape-shifting. For me, taking action has its roots in Grand Street. Here are the ingredients for doing more and saying less:

- Vodka: a chameleon base, it can become whatever you want it to.
- Splash of water: it will create smoothness without changing character.
- Blueberries: powerful antioxidants, they build your immune system and are anti-inflammatory, so they keep things healthy and calm.
- Italian lemon ice: it helps to keep things cool, is refreshing,

and can help relieve a hangover if things don't go well. It's also a nod to my old, bold neighborhood.

- Twist of risk: because if you don't leap you don't know what else is possible.
- Dash of action: will demonstrate what is possible.

Here's to throwing elbows!

DETERMINATION:
Working with Assets

THE BAR AT CINCINNATI started to hum as I worked through the spring and into early summer. I had developed an after-dinner crowd, and Andrew and I were talking about creating a lounge atmosphere after the dining room closed on Friday nights. That's why Andrew hired Gina.

Gina was a beautiful dark-eyed girl with a seductive smile, a tiny waist, and an hourglass figure. She always wore a button-down shirt that strained to stay closed. After her first week, the strain won. The waitstaff, gay and straight, was mesmerized by her assets.

Gina was an aspiring actress and something of a space cadet. On her first day she stood at the service end of the bar and called out her drink order. I politely asked her not to do that, because I knew she was there. I could see it in the faces of my male customers: the "asset stare" gave it away. The guys were dazed, nodding like bobbleheads in the rear window of a gypsy cab.

I explained which glasses were used for different drinks, and how she should set the glasses up for me on a tray with her drink ticket and then come back for them. I told Gina that this was how we kept things running smoothly. She agreed to "try."

"Try" meant that, with the waiting list growing for a table and everyone helping one another keep pace, Gina left her drink trays for the hostess to serve. On Tuesday nights, when it was quiet in the dining room, Gina still left her drink trays for the hostess to serve. Gina didn't tip out anything for the extra help and stopped saying "Thank you" after the second day. "Try" meant that the rest of the waitstaff did more side work, because Gina couldn't seem to get the hang of refilling sugar bowls and salt and pepper shakers, or folding napkins. Even the barback-busboy Bruno got tired of her. If a customer dropped a fork, Gina called for Bruno. If a tray was too heavy to carry down to the dining room, she called for Bruno. If a fly passed by her nose, she called for Bruno.

On her fifth night, Gina decided to leave early. After she left, the waitstaff had a meeting among themselves about what to do about her. They decided that I should talk to Andrew, because I had some influence, having pushed my way into working there. I told them that it wasn't my battle. If they had a problem, they should call a meeting. I had Gina doing what I had asked. Marco was furious. "Just wait: it will come around to you, too, big-time." He motioned for everyone to leave, and no one said good night.

Soon after the Marco hex, it became apparent that in addition to looking for an acting job—maybe instead of—Gina was looking for a guy with a wallet. There were many good-looking men who frequented the bar, but Ian had the best suits. The problem was that Ian was married to Trish, a pretty, overweight, nice gal who was also a fiery drunk.

Ian and Trish were nightly regulars. Trish's back was to the service end of the bar. She was eating oysters Rockefeller, drinking an amber beer, and asking Ian about their upcoming weekend in the Hamptons. Ian, who was staring past Trish at Gina's assets, ran his fingers through his hair, straightened his tie, and didn't answer. Trish turned around slowly, saw the assets, and kicked Ian in the shin. This wasn't the first time that the stare brought out the self-grooming instinct in men and violence in women. Trish excused herself to go to the ladies' room. With bat radar, Gina walked right over to Ian and introduced herself.

"Wow, I love your accent! Are you from California or something?" She smiled her best Gina smile.

"No, the UK." Silence. Ian tried again. "London."

"Oh," Gina purred. "A foreigner! I just loooove foreigners." And with that, another button of her blouse magically opened. I was getting really annoyed and had to do something before Trish came back. I tried to get Gina to collect her loaded tray of drinks. With the back of her hand she motioned for the hostess, all the while engaging Ian.

"Nice suit. What do you do?"

"I'm a financial consultant."

"What?"

"I help companies manage their money." Ian seemed to quickly pick up that assets occupied much of Gina's cerebral blood flow.

"Oooh, a guy who understands money," she cooed. "That's sexy."

Ian was blushing when Trish came out of the restroom wearing fresh lipstick.

"Gina, please move your drinks, NOW." My volume didn't rise but the venom must have, because both Ian and Gina turned to look at me. I nodded toward Trish approaching the bar, and Ian quickly shut down the flirtation. I was at the service end when Gina picked up her drinks. In a tone I hadn't heard before, she said, "Mind your own fucking business," and left before I could say a word.

ADVICE: Things are not always what they seem. Be determined to look beyond visible assets.

Apparently, in Gina's case, there was more above the collarbone than I had originally thought. She was cunning and calculating; it seemed to me that her plan was to do as little as possible, seduce tips with undone buttons, and find someone to "subsidize" her acting career.

One night she pushed the Ian seduction to the point of Trish's getting ugly drunk. I had to ask Ian to take his wife home, whereupon Marco raced to the end of the bar to sneer at me, "I told you so."

It was time to talk with Andrew.

At the end of my shift, while pouring Andrew a cognac, I presented the business case: The tables in the dining room didn't turn over as quickly because Bruno was too busy helping Gina. She had the hostess tied up delivering her drinks. Gina spent more time flirting in the bar than checking on her tables. Her antics were upsetting the female patrons. Overall dinner receipts were down.

Andrew put down his glass and turned toward his office, saying as he went, "I am not going to fire Gina. Deal with it."

This didn't make sense. Andrew was meticulous about his business. The food, décor, personnel, all had to meet his exacting standards, which got higher every month. Why would he keep someone who obviously didn't belong there?

As I thought about Gina, and Andrew's response, I realized there was something I wasn't seeing. Sometimes employees are in positions where they do not appear to have the necessary skills, personality, or common sense to do their jobs. However, their value can come from less visible assets: unusual know-how, a soon-to-be-needed experience base, network connections, or a well-placed relative. Gina must have had another asset I didn't know about, an important one for Andrew.

To me, it didn't matter what the reason was. Andrew wasn't firing Gina, and we needed her out.

Was I going to bully her out? No. Pat had taught me that managing with civility delivered a better payoff than directing with aggression. I decided to tread Pat's path and channel my civility, and determination, into ingenuity. I was going to act, not whine. I was going to get Gina to leave because she wanted to.

And I was going to use Gina's not-so-hidden agenda to help me do it. I figured that improving her life would come from either a director giving her a part or a wealthy man sharing his wallet. I couldn't do anything about the first option, but maybe I could help with the second.

Since Andrew had hired Gina when we were thinking of creating a weekend lounge, I thought maybe it was time to start the venture and get her to do the job that she was originally hired to do. Gina didn't like the idea, having never met a cocktail that she cared to serve, until I told her about all the good-looking guys who came in on Friday nights to wait out the traffic to the Hamptons.

The first time Gina worked on Friday night, she floundered. Thinking sexy was the dress code, she wore a pair of heels and a short skirt. By expecting me to deliver her drinks, which I didn't, she lost customers, who gave up and came to the bar. When she finally started picking up her drink trays, she couldn't deliver one without spilling it somewhere or on someone.

Two weeks later our regular customers from the neighborhood, "The Five Guys," came in with a friend from the Jersey Shore. They were known as the Five Guys because they always came in together—not four or three, always five. I met them my first night auditioning for the job at Cincinnati. They had come in after the dining room had closed and stopped to chat with Andrew on their way out. I lured them back with she-crab soup, dessert, coffee, and cordials. I had seen them nearly every week since.

We were busy, and Gina was a bit frazzled.

"I can't do this. I'm going to ask Andrew to take me off this shift."

"You're doing great," I said. "Can you get their order?" I pointed to the Five Guys, who had just arrived with their friend.

"Are you insane? I have enough trouble getting to my own tables."

"Check out the guy with them. Nice tan and an expensive watch."

Gina looked across the bar and considered him. I saw the gleam in her eye. "I'll do this for you this one time, but then you owe me one."

Gina took their drink order. The Jersey Shore guy's eyes followed her back to the bar. He thanked her when she delivered the drinks and kept watching her all night.

Three weeks later Gina quit Cincinnati, saying that she had found a better opportunity in a beach community. We all celebrated. Strangely, none more than Andrew.

"I knew you'd figure something out." Andrew motioned for the bottle of cognac.

"What do you mean?"

"You don't take no for an answer. I knew that when I said I wouldn't fire her, you'd find a way for her to leave." He had a playful glint in his eyes.

"You set me up."

"No, I fed your fire. Who do you think told the Five Guys to bring their Jersey Shore friend into the lounge?" He lifted his glass. "To everyone getting what they wanted."

Leadership Is More Than Management

Creating the greatest good for all people involved is an art form. It takes the belief that everyone can be satisfied—and can win. Having that kind of view demands an understanding of the many moving parts and people in the interconnected systems of an organization—specifically, understanding the full talents and hidden assets of the human system and bringing the best of them to bear in a quiet and deliberate way. People are more than their résumés. They have experiences and talents that may not come through on a résumé. Managers can be good at recognizing talent, and they might even have a full view of the system—how actions and reactions are connected and effective—but leaders *have* to have this intuitive ability. Leaders have to not only use the right people in the right ways but also provide them with what they need to be successful so that the organization can be successful.

Andrew knew my determination. And, having watched me work for six weeks, he knew that I was committed to engaging people with a smile, a level head, and an encouraging word, regardless of their moods. He knew that I wouldn't try to embarrass or shame Gina into quitting and that, given the right circumstance, I would try to find a way to make it work. That's why he agreed to open the lounge a month before he intended to, and that was also why, when the Five Guys came in one night when I wasn't working, Andrew asked them if they had any single friends who lived out of the area.

Determination comes in many flavors. It can be:

- proactive: taking initiative to find my perfect bartending job;
- reactive: offering to bartend for free to prove my skill when I was initially rejected; or

- radioactive: crying discrimination when Andrew first told me he wouldn't hire a female bartender and trying to force my way into the job. This alternative, the dark side of determination, might have gotten me what I wanted, but with a lot of casualties, a zero-sum game.

Sometimes radioactive determination is a pathway for breaking through ill-conceived barriers. While others may benefit from the groundbreaker's efforts, they are often bruised by people doubting their true capabilities. They find it difficult to attract mentors and may never fit in.

―――――

There were few women strategy consultants in the early eighties. To break into the executive suite, I began by using my initials—"H.N."— instead of my given name. At first my fees were lower than my male counterparts', or I included more activities in proposals at no additional cost. It took some time for me to feel equal to them, even though I knew I was. It took a lot of effort to manage my resentment, to hinder the radioactivity, and to channel that energy into the determination to be better.

Sometimes leaders need to play hardball, but if in so doing they create resentment and alienation, in the long term they may lose more than they gain. Determination and civility are leadership ingredients for achieving the best outcomes, even when some of those outcomes require difficult choices.

Doug Conant, a former CEO of Campbell Soup Company, became the company's leader during very difficult financial times. He had a practice of sending handwritten notes to people in order to recognize them for actions large and small. People cherished his short but thoughtful postcards, which created a culture of appreciation. They felt that their efforts mattered. When it became apparent that restructuring and layoffs were required to turn the company around, Conant was forthcoming with his employees. While the restructuring could have created a toxic corporate atmosphere, Conant's style, his recognition of the small things that make a company tick, and his determination to bring about change with civility kept the company from becoming radioactive.

For Gina, working at Cincinnati was a proactive determination to meet the person who would change her life. Finding a way to get Gina to leave was reactive determination, and I was committed to doing so without the situation becoming radioactive. If I or the staff had tried to use aggression to get Gina to quit by making her life miserable, she could have turned around and made life very difficult for Andrew. After Gina left, Andrew confided in me that a relative of Gina's was an investor in the restaurant business. If we had pushed her out nastily, that funding connection would have vanished. Civility and ingenuity made a better recipe for achieving the best outcome where everyone gained.

After the Bar

Sometimes Visible Assets Are All There Are

Sometimes we need to look behind what is presented and dig deeper into a person's behavior than what we see. Other times a person is showing you all that they are. It is up to you to not fall into a perceptual trap and attribute other qualities to that person that do not exist. If you are determined to read people and situations correctly so that you can respond correctly, then you need patience and curiosity to develop the fine art of understanding what is before you.

The energy industry began deregulating on the West Coast in the early 1990s. Utility companies that had never played in a competitive arena needed to learn how to do so, and quickly. Ben Gilad, the reigning expert on competitive intelligence, was contracted by a utility to analyze competitors and the business environment and to discover and train a director who would report findings directly to the president. As he had with Kellogg, Ben charged me with creating shadow teams to track competitors and new technologies.

The shadow teams were made up of employees selected by their managers. Two categories of people were chosen: altruistic or political. Altruistic members were selected because their knowledge and skill rendered them valuable contributors. Political participants were there to keep their managers informed of what was going on and what people from other parts of the company were saying. Each cross-functional team had five people and was charged with discovering competitors' technology strategies. Specifically, they were attempting to identify what types of processes and capabilities competitors were developing through patent research, hiring practices, and the purchase of companies. This was tricky, because the teams needed to gather publicly available information as well as firsthand knowledge by talking with their colleagues, experts in the field, suppliers, research partners, and anyone else who might know something of value. For instance, some companies claimed in their annual reports to be deep into the latest energy-saving or exploration developments, but they had no new patents pending or the cash flow to fund research. Others were increasing their intellectual stock with new PhDs and industry notables in order to bolster their research acumen or to create expertise in a yet-unpursued area of inquiry. The teams had to collect data, conduct analyses, and figure out "so what" questions—what a competitor could realistically do and what they were likely to do. In addition to their regular jobs, the teams had to dedicate half their time to this competitive intelligence activity for three months.

Working with the director of strategy, I configured the teams, trained them, and coached them through the analytical period. The utility company's intention was to keep the teams working together and to select a director of competitive analysis from among them.

On one team, everyone except Anna was excited to be working with Nate. A lacrosse player from an Ivy League college, an outfielder on the company softball team, and a runner, Nate was a charming and funny extrovert. The others on the team didn't know him personally, but they had witnessed his savvy presentation skills and easy manner at company functions. Since Nate was persuasive and clever and had a sharp wit, the team wanted to appoint him the lead. But Nate diverted the job to Anna. Having worked with her before, Nate cited her great organizational skill. The team thought, *Great guy.* However, as the only person on the team who had actually worked with Nate before, Anna knew he was not what people thought. But she also knew that Nate's popularity would make it impossible for her to decline. Leading this project would be an administrative nightmare. Just the thought of the time it would take to create meetings to accommodate the schedules of four other people made her head swim. And knowing Nate's work style gave her a sinking feeling. Anna asked to meet with me. Everyone had a desk full of work in addition to this very visible assignment.

Eighteen months earlier, Nate and Anna had worked on another project. Anna had created an action plan with the delivery date in mind and divided up the work between them. Nate never had his share done for their meetings. He claimed to be busy, apologized, and always shot his winning smile. After the first missed deadline, the smile worked. After the second, it didn't, and by the third Anna realized that the only way the work would get done was if she did it herself. And she did. The project was delivered on time, and their manager asked to meet with them. Here, Nate took over, presenting the information as if it were all his brainchild. Anna barely got in a word. One week later Nate was promoted. And now here they were, working together on a high-visibility project. She was determined not to have the same thing happen to her this time but didn't know what to do.

I suggested that we structure the work so that Nate's slacking would become apparent to the entire team. If she called him out now, at the beginning, people might sense sour grapes from his having gotten promoted over her. We divided the work into rotating partners and segments. Every three weeks Nate and Anna would be paired with a different person across the project span. If he truly was a slacker and taking advantage of Anna, the team would know.

True to form, when I met with each pairing, Nate was all smiles and presentation, and his partner seemed to quietly fume. When the others worked with Anna, there was a good exchange of ideas and some impressive analytical leaps.

The week before the executive event, I had all the teams present to me first. Anna's team had good information and some good insights but had not created a cohesive *This is what it all means* punch line. And I told them so. Anna and the team, except for Nate, who was "previously committed," met every day after work and over the weekend, determined to impress. And they did: Anna's team had the best results of all the teams. And while each person had a role in presenting at the executive event, Nate took over, appearing to be the driver behind their brilliance.

Without consulting with me first, the director of strategy invited

Nate to be the new director of competitive analysis. Of course Nate accepted. Another promotion for the stylish guy with the bright smile. Anna and her team were surprisingly relieved: Nate's exit trumped their disappointment at not getting the new job.

A month later I got a call from the director of strategy. He wanted to know what other newly appointed directors of competitive analysis did in their first month. I gave him a list of deliverables, which I could tell were news to him. He asked me to come back and coach Nate. I told him it was a waste of time and money. Nate was articulate, smooth, and clever, but he was not analytical or a team player. After a long conversation—the one we should have had before he selected Nate—he appointed Anna as the new director of competitive analysis and returned Nate to his former position. He later became a director of sales.

The director of strategy was determined to launch his competitive intelligence capability with flash. However, his determination overshadowed good leadership practice. Instead of seeking out information about all the players before selecting someone to lead the intelligence focus, he chose the one who seemed to shine. But Nate was a showman, not a deep thinker—persuasive and good at stealing the limelight, but not analytical. His assets were visible, but there was nothing else under the surface. The director of strategy ultimately realized the best use of those attributes was in sales.

Managers, leaders, and employees never have enough time, so they rely on experiences and perceptions to make decisions quickly. We create schemata or mental maps of how we believe the world works. We file information into mental folders to create an impression of whom or what we are engaging with. That's why smart people can make less-than-optimal choices when relying on surface impressions. That's why it is easy to be charmed by visible assets.

Even people with little but their visible assets can have hidden agendas. These can be harmless, like Gina's working as a waitress to meet Mr. Big; or purposeful, like Andrew's hiring Gina to have access to resources; or potentially harmful, like Nate's acting as if he were an analytical whiz. Leaders need to not be swayed by first impressions or perceptual cues. They need the fortitude and determination to dig deeper, to invest more precious time into understanding people, places, and things, and to go beyond visible assets.

The Drink

UNDER THE HOOD

This is a sweet three-layered after-dinner drink in a chilled pony glass. In order:

1 peach slice
½ tablespoon crème de cassis
½ tablespoon Galliano
½ tablespoon peach liqueur
¾ ounce vodka
2 Maraschino cherries, skewered

Enjoy layering the first four ingredients before adding the vodka. Dress with two Maraschino cherries skewered by a toothpick and placed sideways across the top of the glass, peeking through the floating top layer. Rim with determination. Add a splash of civility. Serve neat.

Liqueurs come in a variety of flavors and molecular weights; this makes it possible to layer them, creating depth. Determination also comes in different flavors and molecular weights. Proactive and reactive determination can be topped with aggression or civility. Radioactive determination is aggressive and, when combined with other ingredients, can become a big black volatile hole that is very hard to climb out of.

Any flavor of determination can breed ingenuity. The greatest good for all is more likely to occur when determination is layered with civility and ingenuity. Having Gina serve cocktails on Friday night to find a new boyfriend so she would leave on good terms, and having Andrew add the secret ingredient—the Jersey Shore guy—created layering so there was something for everyone.

- Vodka: it is an invisible creator of balance.
- Peach liqueur: the lightest in weight, it can be almost too sweet, but it is pretty.
- Galliano: gold in color and made from herbs, it is known for digestive properties. It's good after a large meal or a complex project.
- Crème de cassis: the heaviest in weight, it is another digestive, created by French monks. It is also thought to cure wretchedness, and perhaps needed if the layering was especially difficult!
- Peach slice: for sweetness—civility after wretchedness.
- Maraschino cherries: the more you drink, the larger they become; the more you know, the more you see.
- Rim with determination: there are many ways to make things happen.
- Serve neat to let the layers play out on their own.

Here's to everyone getting what they want (for the greatest good of all)!

3

VISION: Turn On the Lights

ONE SUMMER ANDREW CLOSED Cincinnati during the slowest two weeks of the season, so I went backpacking in Europe. I returned a few days after Cincinnati reopened. The softly lit elegant eatery with the pink walls now had white subway tile and black and orange accents. The dining room tables had become booths, and instead of white cloths, brown paper now covered them. In the corner of the waiters' stand were mallets and stacks of glass bowls. The place smelled like cloves, pepper, and beer.

When I walked in, I thought I was in the wrong place. I had been working at Cincinnati for two years and could get there with my eyes closed, but I walked outside to check the street signs and look at the façade. And that's when I saw it: a gigantic orange hard-shell crab and "Maryland Crab House" painted on a clear plate-glass window. Our mystique had been replaced with garishness. My perfect place, with the soft music and sexy lighting, now played Waylon Jennings and looked like a cafeteria.

Andrew had secretly planned this new place with a new menu for months. There were some holdovers from Cincinnati, but the

Maryland Crab House was now a Chesapeake Bay boardwalk experience. Not only did Andrew not share his vision for the new restaurant but even after it opened he never held a meeting to explain the new menu to the staff. Marco told me that all Andrew did do was demonstrate the new table set.

"Eating hard-shell crabs is very different than lobster," Marco said as he went over to the service station, grabbed a piece of brown paper, a wood mallet, a small wood board, and a tiny fork. He folded the paper to fit the bar and motioned for Bruno.

"Hey, can you fetch me one of those hard-shells? I think Helen needs to see this for herself."

Bruno came over, gave me a hug hello, and said, "You're going to freak."

He came back with a steamed hard-shell crab the size of my open hand covered in Old Bay seasoning. He placed it on the board, which was on top of the brown paper with a stack of white paper napkins.

Marco sat down, picked up the mallet, and began smashing the crab. Pieces flew. Then he picked up a leg, and with the tiny fork tried to get the meat out. His hands were covered in spices, so he licked his fingers. Disgusted, he stood up, wiping his hands on a wad of napkins.

"This is our new reality, a violent mess. I don't know how you're going to do this at the bar. People literally suck and bite and smash the shit out of these things. After they're done, you give them a little finger bowl to clean their hands. They wash it down with some Baltimore brew that tastes like dishwater. Their glasses get filthy, so you'll be washing more. The whole thing is asinine, if you ask me."

"How are the regulars taking it?" I asked.

"Most aren't back from their summer retreats. What they might like even less than the menu change are all the people from out of the neighborhood who are flocking here. These crabs are a religion for people who move north of the Mason-Dixon Line. Problem is, the tables turn slower if they eat these things, and beer is cheaper than bourbon."

I was in shock. How could such a big change have been carried out on the sly?

That night, after closing out the register, I sat down with Andrew. He was enjoying the new customers and the bewildered staff. I asked him why he hadn't shared the new restaurant design with any of us beforehand. His response was simple: he didn't want to listen to anyone whine about it. I saw his point. Most people don't like change. But I believed that we all would be working better if we had been a part of it. How could I talk to people about the cuisine? Andrew said that the people coming in knew what this food was all about. As for the regulars, he kept some of their favorites and felt that "they'll get used to it."

I wasn't convinced. At the Gable Inn, Pat had increased receipts by getting people to have dinner at the bar. When a new chef joined the crew and created specials that people were unfamiliar with, like blackened redfish, Pat not only learned how to describe the item but also, when the bar was full, would get samples to pass around. People were more likely to try something new if they understood what it was. Knowledge was courage.

But Andrew had left us to find our way in the dark. He figured that we would learn the menu by serving knowledgeable consumers. I asked the cooks to let us sample the specials. But the majority of the menu, and how to crack the hard shells, was still a mystery to us when the regulars returned. And they were not happy with the décor, the music, the menu, or all the folks coming in from outside of the neighborhood. They stuck with what they knew, the few items Andrew kept from Cincinnati. And they stopped dining with us as often.

A week later, help came from a most unlikely place: a new customer named James, who had been transferred from his company's home office in Baltimore to Manhattan. On a cooler-than-usual Friday, he had chosen to walk home and was drawn into our place by the crab in the window. He sat at the bar, we introduced ourselves, and he ordered a Maryland-brewed beer. He asked to see the menu. His face lit up. "Y'all really have hard-shells here! I see the paper on the tables. Can I order a half dozen at the bar?"

These were the words I had been dreading. It meant that I would have to paper his space and change his glass at least three times. And he would sit there forever banging, picking, and sucking. To make the best of it, I watched and took mental notes.

With deliberate and expert hands, James dismembered the first crab. Ian, the regular originally from Britain, was sitting on his usual stool and waved me over.

"Who's the guy surgically removing the sweet meat over there?"

I introduced him to James. Ian walked over to shake James's hand, but it was covered in spice and spit, so instead he offered a short bow. Then he stood over James's shoulder to watch as he started in on the second one.

"Fascinating. There's nothing like this in the UK. Are they spicy?"

"Not spicy, flavorful," James said, and blushed. I sensed that he was not used to being the center of attention.

"Whatever that means. How hard do you need to spank the little buggers?"

I was walking over to shoo Ian away when James solved the problem for himself.

"Why not get an order and I'll coach you through it?"

"Really good man, a splendid idea. Helen, bring it on, and one of those watery beers as well. When in Rome . . ."

For the next hour the two crab crackers at the bar banged, smashed, and ate their way into their new reality. James was methodical and exact in breaking his crabs. Ian mangled, twisted, left a mess, and was a mess. But James's enthusiasm for the crabs was contagious and he demonstrated that others could learn his culinary technique. The bar crowd grew with people studying James's method. I surveyed the mini-circus unfolding in front of me. All it had taken to transmute resistance into excitement was knowing how to dismember a crab, to be part of the change. Becoming an insider, not an outsider.

Building a community at the bar meant that the bartender needed to bring people into a story so that they could feel included. When there was a party in the dining room at the Gable Inn, the bar would get slammed with thirty or forty drink orders at once, which meant that the regulars had to wait. But when Pat or I gave them a few words about a bridal shower or funeral or family gathering, they became part of the story. Being included on the inside scoop was enough for them to patiently wait for their turn to get served. A little knowledge carried a lot of power.

When our restaurant changed, the regulars felt excluded, inade-quate, because they didn't know how to crack hard-shells. Once they felt like insiders and could participate and master the crab-eating technique, they became more adventurous with the new menu. They started eating with us more often—again.

Yet the shock of the change left me a bit off my game. I felt betrayed, confused, and hurt. Over the previous two years at Cincinnati, Andrew and I had planned and implemented change together. We had created the weekend lounge, Sunday brunch, snowstorm parties. With this change, the most important one, he had left me on the outside. I had considered myself more of Andrew's partner, and now I was just the bartender. I had viewed Cincinnati as a place where I could build a bar scene and my management chops. I had taken ownership of my work and pride in my accomplishments. I thought that meant something to Andrew. I took my new outsider status personally.

Andrew's not sharing his plan also made it hard for me to deliver the type of bar experience I wanted to. I couldn't serve the community I was building because I wasn't privy to the new knowledge. It hurt my credibility. I wished that Andrew had taught me how to handle the hard-shell crabs or that I had pushed him to do so. I could have made it an adventure. He might not have wanted to listen to us whine, but I had to listen to our customers complain about being left in the dark and try to convince them that there would be a light. The only saving grace was that we were all in the same boat. This didn't make Andrew, the common enemy, look good. Thankfully, James had showed up to turn on the lights when I couldn't and Andrew wouldn't.

ADVICE: A good manager can get things done in the dark. A good leader turns on the lights.

Two weeks after James's tutorial, Andrew saw five people at the bar with mallets and his face lit up. "Told you so," he said. He was giddy with the attention that the restaurant was getting. "We needed to distinguish ourselves from the other neighborhood places with something other than having the most expensive menu. I love this food and no one else is doing it. There are enough southerners in New York to seek us out. Now we can be a destination as well as a neighborhood place."

It was a savvy business move. Andrew understood that he needed to differentiate to attract people from outside Gramercy Park. He had been dreaming of this type of restaurant since he came to New York. He waited until he had built a good enough reputation to be reviewed and had secured a supply of hard-shell crabs.

Although the Maryland Crab House was a big success, it was not making big-success money. Andrew studied the receipts. As Marco had said, National Bohemian beer was cheaper than bourbon. At Cincinnati we had sold mostly cocktails and imported beer.

So Andrew created a wine list to complement the menu. Bottles of wine can have a 100 percent markup, a big plus for the waitstaff and the nightly receipts. But in the first two weeks, we sold only ten bottles.

Andrew called a staff meeting on a Sunday between brunch and the dinner hour.

"Why aren't you selling more wine?"

"Because people like to gargle with that Maryland beer when they are sucking their fingers clean," Marco said. "We're all working harder and making less money. And another thing"—Marco was a dam bursting—"we are sick of you treating us like two-year-olds and springing this type of shit on us. Now we have a wine list. Big deal! None of us have a clue what the wine is, what to pair it with, or how to talk about it. How can we sell something we don't understand?" Marco wasn't raising his voice but it was clear that he had had enough. Strangely, he appeared much taller to me that day.

Andrew looked to me for support. Instead, I backed Marco. I told him that some of the anger he was hearing from Marco reflected the hurt we felt by being left out and not trusted to understand his reasoning. We had all felt that our teamwork and our efforts to create an exceptional experience for our customers deserved to be recognized and treated with more respect.

"It was a business decision; it's not personal," Andrew said.

"We take pride in what we do. We care about this place. We help each other. This isn't just business, it *is* personal."

Andrew was quiet for a few moments and then bounded upstairs. We waited for fifteen minutes. Thinking he didn't want to listen to us "whine" anymore, we started toward the door. Instead, he came down with a tray of food and asked me to open bottles from the wine list. We tasted, sipped, and took notes for two hours. Andrew's pairings were terrific. He gave us talking points and a cheat sheet on what to suggest with each type of flavor and texture.

We were now out of the dark and part of the vision. We could promote the menu with confidence. Selling a bottle of wine instead of three beers had us running less and making more. Time and energy, our most important resources, were being invested to bring us larger returns.

Leadership Is More Than Management

Managers have the power to get people to do things because they can reward and punish. Leaders get people to do things because they have the power of permission. People choose to follow either because of the leader's charisma or their shared belief in the vision, or both.

Andrew, the leader, had the vision to bring the restaurant beyond its current station. He realized that an expensive neighborhood restaurant might not flourish during seasonal and economic shifts. A destination restaurant had a greater chance of succeeding financially and attracting reviewer attention. He needed both in order to open another restaurant. This was ambitious and smart, but his unwillingness to share the vision because he didn't want to deal with people "whining" about it was shortsighted and less smart. So what if we whined? If we had been prepared when we opened—if we had known what we were selling—we would have achieved a lot more a lot sooner with a lot less ill will.

Andrew's vision, ingenuity, and determination were leadership qualities; his implementation—not taking action sooner to prepare the staff—was poor management. Successful change demands *both* leadership and good management. The staff needed Andrew to be the great ship in front pointing the way for the rest of the armada.

After the Bar

You Need to Find the Switch

People need to understand what they are selling in order to be good at selling. They want to be regarded as integral pieces of the puzzle. With a clear, directed vision, people can navigate the good that comes with change as well as the challenges. Andrew had clear vision and bad management, but sometimes the opposite can be true: someone can have great management skills and an elusive vision.

Bill Ruh began his career with the Department of Defense (DoD) think tank MITRE Corporation. A brilliant computer engineer and a good and affable manager, he rose quickly through the ranks. Seven years later, he joined Mitretek Systems, a DoD offshoot, as its senior vice president of technology development. Settling near his Virginia office, he rose quickly there, too.

I met Bill at a competitive intelligence conference, an annual gathering of people wanting to learn how to conduct competitive intelligence activities as well as companies looking for new business for their software, information, and reporting services. Consultants and consulting firms offer to conduct competitor and industry analysis, run war games and scenario analysis, engage in special investigative projects, and create intelligence structures. I was there to network and secure a new client. Bill was there to learn about competitive intelligence function. He invited me to McLean to help create a competitive intelligence capability for an offshoot—a for-profit technology start-up that would apply systems engineering to a then-new opportunity: the Internet.

The CEO of the new venture had put Bill in charge of recruiting an array of the best and brightest from his former companies. The move posed a big risk to the new recruits: leave relatively secure jobs for the unknown, and for the chance to build a technology company and own stock. Because of Bill's track record and his charisma, many people who had worked for or with him wanted to join him. Too many, actually. The start-up company, later named Concept Five Technologies, was quickly staffed with more than one hundred people.

The CEO had not articulated a vision and Bill hadn't felt that he was in a position to do so, so I began my assignment by interviewing many of these pioneers to see if an informal vision would emerge. They were settling into offices and talking about when they could go public, but not talking about what exactly Concept Five would become. Yet they shared a multitude of innovative ideas.

Bill and I put people in teams to see if they could converge on a couple of platforms. With their engineers' understanding of the potential of this brave new world, they focused on creating "cool software applications" that businesses could use the Internet for. Their ideas varied: access to cash from bank accounts through machines; credit card purchasing from Internet Web sites; company directories of employees with their résumés, skills, and interests cataloged so that a project could be quickly staffed; knowledge-management software for capturing, codifying, cataloging, and disseminating company reports; gambling; and security. Unfortunately, in the face of uncertainty, the teams became wedded to their ideas, so that, when we brought them together, they found little agreement on a common direction. Each team thought they had the path to success and, without a guiding vision, all paths seemed viable. So instead of working together on one or two ideas, they continued to work on what each thought was the best cool application.

The CEO decided which ideas he and Bill would pitch to corporations. The companies thought that many of the ideas were great concepts but could see nothing tangible for them to buy into. With all of this unharnessed Internet brainstorming and no revenue coming in, Concept Five was burning through its angel funding.

The pioneers mostly had experience with the Department of Defense and the not-for-profit world. Their previous jobs revolved around producing whatever a general from the armed forces asked for, or dreaming up what they should be asking for. Then the money truck would back up to the loading dock, and they had what they needed to create. This mind-set was very different from that of a start-up company burning through cash while chasing too many different ideas in a world without easy access to more money. I suggested we have an off-site meeting with the pioneers to run a visioning session so they could agree on a direction that would help them focus the idea mill. Bill felt that vision was the CEO's purview and not his. So instead we ran a two-and-a-half-day meeting to try to launch the pioneers into a for-profit business mind-set. Using the information I had gathered from interviewing the pioneers, Bill and I worked to develop an organization with people in specific functions: some would identify competitive opportunities, while others narrowed down the product-development focus. Over the next three months I kept in close contact with Bill and the function leaders, but although they were still having cool ideas, product-design money was dwindling, and there still was no vision to unify their efforts.

By the time my work with Concept Five Technologies drew to a close, those who were most nervous about not having a clear focus had left the company and returned to Mitretek and MITRE. Bill was on the road most of the time with the CEO raising money and selling concepts. Eventually Bill focused developer attention on e-business and enterprise software and the company launched a couple of applications. Bill left the company within five years and climbed to new heights across Fortune 500 firms. The CEO never articulated a formal vision for Concept Five Technologies, and although it opened six offices and developed products and services across multiple Internet venues, it never went public and went out of business in 2011.

> *Where there is no vision, the people perish . . .*
> —Proverbs 29:18 (KJV)

Andrew had a vision but chose not to share it with his staff. Concept Five's CEO believed that if he put smart people in a room, they would come up with the vision. And in fact that might work for a big company, creating a Skunk Works and letting a small group of people be innovative. But a start-up by nature is vision driven. It is where a few people come together to build a dream. In Concept Five's case, there were too many smart people wanting to create the next big Internet thing and go public.

Bill did not want to tell his colleagues what they could or couldn't do. Charismatic and well-intentioned, he didn't want to stifle the excitement. But what was needed most was a beacon to direct everyone's talent. When the money ran low and people became nervous, Bill took the reins and emerged as the leader.

While Andrew had the vision and needed to turn on the lights, Bill had the switch on without a bulb in the socket. Not sharing the vision, keeping people in the dark, can have unintended consequences. Bill was surprised to find his people pulling in different directions. He wound up spending most of his time putting out fires and trying to raise money instead of leading the applications design effort. He lost his most talented people when they felt as if funding would run out before they could attach their efforts to a winning product.

The unintended consequence of my feeling betrayed by not knowing about the restaurant change in advance was as much my own stumble in the dark as Andrew's. Andrew wanted to be expedient. He didn't intend to be hurtful. During my time working for him, he welcomed my suggestions and relied on me as a sounding board. We introduced change together. My willingness to be more involved in the management of the restaurant was my choice. And if I was going to engage, to give of my time, energy, and heart, then I needed to do so without strings attached, without the expectation that I would always be included in decision-making.

Andrew's choice to change the restaurant without including me in the planning wasn't personal. I chose to take it that way. *I* wasn't being slighted—we *all* were. I wasn't understanding the motivation behind Andrew's behavior. I was assuming that, because he had included me in some decision-making, he always would, and that if he didn't this time it was because I had done something to change his behavior. But it was Andrew, not me. He was making a choice based on the situation. If I had seen it this way, instead of licking my wounds, I could have been more persistent in getting Andrew to teach us how to crack a crab. I could have done more sooner to transform a bad situation into a better one.

I had a similar opportunity to transform the situation with Bill Ruh. I could have tried to push him to create a vision with the pioneers, regardless of whether the CEO thought it was time to do so. Different types of leaders generate action. Some are formal: they have titles and defined roles and the power to allocate budgets and get things done through people. That was the CEO at Concept Five Technologies. Others are informal: they have authority because people want to do what they ask. They do it not because they are concerned about their annual reviews or their bonuses but because they believe in that person, their sensibilities, the project at hand. That was Bill.

Here's why I didn't push. Bill felt he was being given the opportunity of a lifetime: to create a company that would not only advance society through new technologies but also provide a means for his colleagues and friends to do interesting work; if the company went public, it could bring them all a big payday. When I asked Bill about his vision, about doing it whether the CEO mandated it or not, he shut me down. It was a line he was not willing to cross: to go behind the back of the CEO, the person who was giving him this great opportunity. In his mind that would have been disloyal. He had a blind spot. And because of that, nothing I could say would move him. Instead we tried to shift the culture and mind-set of those who came along to Concept Five. Not an ideal situation, but one that did find some legs for almost twenty years.

You have to be willing to see to have vision.

Managing in the dark sets people up to stub their toes or bump into walls. Darkness creates anxiety. Turning on the light directs energy into creative and productive pursuits.

The Drink

MARYLAND COMFORT

Start with a surfside vision: the smell of salty air, a boardwalk, the sound of waves, a seagull gliding.

2 ounces of bourbon

Stir into the bourbon a pinch of clove and cinnamon and cardamom

2 tablespoons ginger beer

Blend in communication. Shake over ice. Serve neat. (Old Bay–seasoned steamed hard-shell crab optional.)

Vision is a driver. Organizations have visions that serve to pull everyone in the same direction. Departments can have visions that align how priorities are set. People have visions that guide choice among competing activities. Andrew had a vision to create surfside ambience in Gramercy Park and then opened a second concept restaurant to establish himself as a restaurateur. I had a vision to get off Grand Street and become a professional. A dream creates movement. And, despite setbacks, determination to achieve vision pushes one foot in front of the other. Vision mixes action, determination, and ingenuity into various cocktails.

- Vision: the long view, it is a deliberate march into the light.
- Bourbon: associated with the South, it is corn changed into spirit and then colored by aging in charred oak barrels for years. It takes time and patience.
- Clove: warm and aromatic, it has a numbing effect to manage pain, which can be attached to change.

- Cinnamon: warm and aromatic, it is thought to manage blood sugar and metabolism, and supports the eyes (that is, vision).
- Cardamom: seeds in a pod, they are pungent and thought to relieve congestion (getting stuck) and neutralize odor (when things go bad) and basically help you digest it all.
- Ginger beer: recommended for nausea, joint pain, and headache, it also tastes really good and can help when things get tough.
- Communication: before is usually better than after.

Here's to the road ahead!

ADVICE FOR LEADERSHIP

4

INTEGRITY: Own What's Yours

IT WAS A FULL moon, that time when characters fill emergency rooms, police stations, and bars. Something about its gravitational pull causes the tide to swell and makes people nutty or brilliant. It was also a blue moon, and we at the Crab House were preparing ourselves.

"Tonight's blue moon is the second full moon this month—one extra time for the crazies to crawl out from under their rocks and howl. I'm talking double-down lunatics. Keep a close eye on those crab forks!" Marco said, laughing, sort of.

The hostess heard the conversation and piped in: "And Mercury is in retrograde. If you ask me, all bets are off for tonight."

Marco and I turned to look at her. With an audible sigh he asked, "What is a Mercury in retrograde?"

"Retrograde is when a planet appears to be moving backward in the zodiac, something to do with the orbital revolution of the Earth. Anyhow, Mercury is the master communicator, so when in retrograde, it creates communication roadblocks. Don't fight with your friends, sign any contracts, or travel too far from home," she said, holding up a finger for each possibility. "Different things can happen. People dig in their heels and become really stubborn about nonsense. They are subject to events out of their control. Or they can open their minds to new thinking."

I was glad that she wasn't lifting any more fingers. Marco was visibly unnerved.

"Great, we're going to have customers throwing mallets at each other across the table, ordering one thing when they really wanted another, tipping like crap," he said. He turned to storm away and ran directly into Bruno.

"What's up, Marco? You're upset and the shift hasn't even started yet!"

"Blue moon and Mercury in retrograde! I should have called in sick."

"*I see a bad moon a-rising . . .*" Bruno started singing the classic Creedence Clearwater Revival song. Marco gave him a dirty look and told him to shut up. Bruno called Marco a drama queen and they stalked off to opposite ends of the dining room.

I figured I could deal with one more night with a full moon, but this Mercury-in-retrograde thing would last three weeks.

That night we got slammed. Wait time for a table was nearly an hour. The kitchen was down a person. The ice maker was on the fritz. I had the service area loaded with trays and people three-deep at the bar. Marco had a guy at his table who didn't like the Chablis he had ordered from the wine list, so he came back to the bar to get a different bottle.

"Here, sell this by the glass. There's nothing wrong with it, but the Neanderthal said it was sour."

"How do you know that it's not?" I asked. I thought I was asking this innocently, but Marco took offense.

"Do I tell you how to do your job? Do I question you about your drinks? No. So don't give me any shit and just give me the Chardonnay."

I ignored his cranky self and gave him the bottle, and off he went. Pat had shown me that we could let a lot of waitstaff histrionics slide. "Think of it as water rolling off a duck's back. It's meaningless, and if you play into it, it can only escalate. Don't take it personally and it won't become personal."

Five minutes later Marco was back. His dislike of the Neanderthal and his "cheesy" girlfriend was increasing. He was holding the bottle of Chardonnay I had just given him and now demanded the sauvignon blanc. Not knowing Andrew's policy when these things happened, because they rarely did, and wanting to get Marco and his aggression out of my face, I handed him the bottle. He was back a few minutes later asking for the Merlot. I decided that if after three bottles of wine the Neanderthal couldn't find something he liked, he would have to pay for it from now on. I already had expensive wine I was selling by the glass at tap prices.

I was getting annoyed and worried about how I was going to explain to Andrew the fine wine being sold from the house well. Marco was more annoyed, because he was dealing with the Neanderthal. And the Neanderthal was apparently the most annoyed of all, because he came storming to the bar.

"I am not going to pay for this shitty wine before I taste it!" he shouted. He wore a black wife-beater tank that accentuated his hairy shoulders and neck, which was as big as my thigh.

"Sir, I think you've tried enough bottles to know that you don't like our selection. There's no reason to continue this expedition," I replied. Pat had taught me to always call a customer "sir" when I wanted to call him "jerk," to keep my tone of voice steady, and to squeeze my forefinger and thumb together under the bar to channel the aggression somewhere else.

"You're a bitch, you know that? I don't need this shit."

"Sir, do we serve a beer that you know you enjoy? I would be happy to buy you and your friend a beer to accompany your meal," I said. I wondered if Pat was able to let being called "bitch" roll off her back, because I was having a problem with it. My tone of voice gave me away.

The Neanderthal looked me up and down, as if considering whether he could wring my neck across the bar. I adopted my Grand Street "She crazy" look and posture, elbows ready to fly. Trish whispered to Ian, "Mother of God." Out of the corner of my eye I saw James shift his hold on his mallet. I had to get us all out of this.

Saccharine-sweet, I asked, "Sir, may I get you that beer?"

"No, you can kiss my ass. We're getting out of this dump." He thumped off, grabbed his girl by the arm, and pushed her along. She wanted to stay. He would have no part of it. The plate-glass window shook when he slammed his way out. But he was gone.

"Told you: the blue moon. The creatures from beneath dig their way out," Marco said from the service end of the bar, where he was setting up glasses.

Andrew came in an hour later and spotted the three open bottles of wine from the wine list in the service well. He walked over to the service end.

"What are those bottles doing there?"

"They're from the dining room."

"Three tables sent back wine in one night?"

"No, we had a challenging customer who didn't like anything."

"So why are there three bottles?" He wasn't raising his voice, but I could almost see the hair on the back of his neck rise.

"We kept trying to find a bottle that he would like."

"You're kidding me, right?"

"It happened really fast and I wasn't sure what to do. Finally, when he asked for a fourth bottle, I told him he'd have to pay for it."

"What?" Now he was raising his voice and banging his pen on the bar.

"I offered to buy him a beer of his choice. The whole thing didn't go very well, and he and his girlfriend left."

"Without eating?"

"Yes, without eating."

"So you basically screwed the whole thing up!" Andrew said, steaming. He had never spoken to me like that before.

I tried not to react. I took a breath. I went over the four choices I had in my head before I answered him. I could explain that we were getting slammed and that the Neanderthal was menacing; that Marco was not managing his customer and that I didn't know what to do; that he had never articulated a policy about returns; or I could own it as my fault for not managing the situation better. All eyes at the bar were on us.

"I'm sorry, Andrew. I didn't know what to do. I should never have given him the third bottle of wine. I didn't handle it right. I will do it better next time. Is there something I can do now to make it work better?"

Andrew tilted his head and held his tongue. He just stared at me, huffed, and went upstairs.

ADVICE: Don't get caught up in what isn't yours, but if you do, own it.

"Wow, you ate all that up yourself," Ian said as he handed me a bottle of antacids from his pocket.

"I made bad choices."

"I saw the whole thing. It was really busy and there was a lot going on. It's not all your fault." He was being protective, and Trish nodded in agreement.

"At any time I could have stopped the game. I didn't. I am in control of the liquor supply, so it is mine to own."

Marco waved me over to the service end and thanked me for not throwing him under the bus. He walked away singing, *"Blue moon / You saw me standing alone . . ."* That made me smile.

We finished the shift with four orders of food sent back to the kitchen, two broken mallets, a missing umbrella stand, and not a clean apron in the house.

"I have never felt so dirty in my life," Marco said, pulling off his apron and taking a seat at the bar. "We survived the night. Let me have some of that wine."

"I sold it all."

"Well, that's good, at least. How about an amber draft?"

Andrew came downstairs with a small chalkboard and a list. He looked at Marco and then me.

"I figured it was your station."

"Don't start, Andy. It's been a hell of a shift."

"Here's what we do next time. If someone returns a bottle of wine, and if you're sure that it hasn't spoiled, sell it by the glass as a tasting special. Helen, you put the name of the wine and the price per glass on this chalkboard. I made a price list for you. If it's corked, leave it for me to decide what to do with it. If the bottle doesn't sell out, send it to the kitchen; they'll cook with it the next day. And if a customer returns a second bottle of wine, *never* offer them a third. I don't care who they are. Instead, offer them a taste of the house wine. If they don't like that, move them to beer or a cocktail, as you rightly tried to do."

We nodded in unison. I appreciated Andrew's letting me know that at least I had done something right. Marco then filled Andrew in on the blue-moon-and-Mercury-in-retrograde whammy. Andrew wasn't buying any of it, but I was thinking that we had twenty more days to go. After Marco left, Andrew got a glass and reached across the bar to serve himself a draft beer.

"That was an adventure."

"Yeah. I'm sorry that I didn't have my head on straight tonight," I said. I was annoyed at myself.

"Don't worry about it. I love that you are not perfect," he said, with the Andrew twinkle that could make me like him when I had sworn to hate him.

"Doing things wrong creates an opportunity for you to do it right the next time. You take a chance: if it doesn't work out, then there's an opening for us all to do it better," he said. Andrew the philosopher. Where did this guy come from? Maybe there really was something behind Mercury in retrograde making people look at the world differently.

"Shit happens," he continued. "You're such a control freak that you think if you make everything your fault, you can fix it. You do need to have the integrity to admit to what is yours, and to try not to make the same mistakes, and you did that. But not all of what happened tonight was yours. Marco is an experienced waiter. He should have known better. Some of it was his. Some of it was mine, not having a policy in place. And some was the customer's. And some was the moon." He winked at me.

I took a deep breath. His words made sense.

"Thanks, Andrew. I get it."

"Don't thank me. Pour me another beer and let's figure out where we'll find clean aprons for tomorrow's shift."

Leadership Is More Than Management

Integrity is easy to define and hard to live. In its full expression, integrity is about being honest in a situation, with others and with yourself, and being honest about the situation and its circumstances. Integrity pushes leaders to see situations for what they are, not what they want them to be. Leaders don't lie to others or themselves. They recognize flaws, and when something doesn't work out, real leaders use the situation as an opportunity to learn.

While Andrew was annoyed, he accepted my ownership of the mistake and my apology, and he realized his part in the problem as well. He owned what was his and used it as an opportunity to elevate his management of the restaurant.

Andrew also recognized who I was. I had worked for him for three years by then, and he knew that I was reliable and well-intentioned but not perfect. And that was okay. Because while striving for perfection is noble, it's also misguided. It can drive achievement and the push for excellence, but it's also a way to try to control your environment, and not everything is in our control.

After the Bar

If There's No One to Tie Your Shoes, Tie Your Own

Astrology aside, sometimes it is hard to achieve alignment, to have your goals and resources in position to support one another. Misalignment can result from someone having a bad day, an order arriving incomplete, a client changing his mind, or the powers that be creating new rules. Whatever the source, when the stars don't align, things may not work out. Good leaders have the integrity not to complain or blame; they have perspective and instead take action.

In the mid-1990s, I was invited to run a retreat for the board of the Anderson School (now the Anderson Center for Autism, in upstate New York), which educates and cares for special-needs children and adults. The board and I shared an off-site day discussing the school's vision and future goals. The long-tenured executive director wanted to rejuvenate the board and elevate the school's potential, perhaps even begin planning for a new school building. Vicki Sylvester was head of the finance committee. She also was the executive director of Community Based Services (CBS), a not-for-profit that ran group homes for autistic and disabled adults in a different county. We clicked at the retreat, and she invited me to work with her agency. Over the years since, I have been her advisor, confidante, and friend.

When I first worked with CBS, it ran five homes in good neighborhoods, each furnished with a designer's flare. The houses were well staffed, the clients beautifully dressed, and their parents part of the CBS extended family. Even though the budget came from various New York State agencies, Vicki had the fund-raising skill and financial acumen to have a surplus in the bank for emergencies.

The first thing Vicki contracted me to do was a climate survey of her staff to discover how they felt about their roles and the agency. In essence, she was asking for feedback about her leadership, and while most of what I heard was extremely positive, whatever came back that wasn't was addressed by Vicki earnestly and professionally. She knew that she couldn't give everyone exactly what they wanted, but she made sure that they had what they needed.

Over fifteen years I worked strategically with CBS on vision, growth, and diversification. The agency grew to eight houses and was considering acquiring more. Then in 2008, with expenses increasing and the economy in recession, the state didn't issue a cost-of-living increase. The state's resources and CBS's commitment to enhance its clients' quality of life were out of alignment.

Instead of cutting services to meet budgetary constraints, however, Vicki innovated. To save money by centralizing food procurement and preparation, Vicky decided to create a commissary, and enlisted her friend Allan, a Culinary Institute of America graduate who ran a successful restaurant near her home, to run it. Allan had just sold his business and had catered many events for her agency and enjoyed interacting with her clients. The commissary employed CBS clients who had the skill level to work there, and Allan taught house managers to create well-balanced and appealing meals.

The financial relief the commissary gave the agency was short-lived, because the first wave of budget cuts hit in 2010. Not getting cost-of-living increases was bad enough, but a decrease in resources posed a direct threat to CBS's dedication to maintaining the quality of their homes and client services. Fund-raising would provide a buffer but not a steady flow of income. We spent hours brainstorming different options for increasing cash flow, and Vicki realized that her best option was to diversify by creating an adult-care day program that other area agency clients could attend. The state funded client participation in these enrichment programs and would provide CBS with an additional revenue stream.

Another big wave of budget cuts in 2014 made it impossible for CBS to maintain the same level of client quality of life. In addition, the state wanted agencies to invest their resources to facilitate client integration into the community, meaning they wanted the disabled to become more productive through employment and, where possible, more independent. There were not many employment options for developmentally and physically challenged people, especially in a recovering economy. Compounding the challenge of operating for years without cost-of-living adjustments were two resource dilemmas: a mandate to invest in productive engagement, and an additional 4 percent decrease in the budget. In three years, with expenses increasing, the agency budget was down 8 percent.

To maintain CBS's integrity and respond to both challenges posed by the state was daunting, but Vicki was determined not to compromise the homes, the attention to detail, or the care that clients and their families had come to rely on. She aimed to augment her budget without relying solely on fund-raising and to provide additional employment opportunities for her clients who were capable of working.

Because the commissary had worked out well, and the clients were good at working with food and packaging, Vicki brainstormed another food-based venture with Allan. They created an all-natural, healthful, delicious dog treats company. (We knew that they were delicious because we all tasted them.) The company is called Good Reasons (www.goodreasons.com). It employs and integrates nondisabled people who are supportive of their disabled coworkers. In addition to enjoying the work of making and packaging dog treats, the clients earn wages. CBS funnels the profits from the venture back into the agency, and both help to sustain client quality of life.

When the stars don't align, when you're thrown a curveball, you can adjust your stance or continue swinging and miss the ball. My swinging at the drama created by Marco and the Neanderthal was a miss. I thought that I was adjusting my stance, treating Marco's heightened anxiety and the Neanderthal's aggression as if they were unimportant. But I wasn't. I was reacting. I could have changed the tone to create better alignment by approaching the customer's table and offering tastings of our house wine, giving him the attention he was after. Instead, I let Marco's drama, from the moment the shift started, grease the ball.

It's okay to not see the curveball coming sometimes, to swing and miss. No one bats a thousand. The opportunity here is to learn from what didn't work and not do the same thing again. There can be more misses, but not at the same pitch. You can't control the ball that is coming, but you can control how you respond.

Vicki's response to the curveball—the state's cutting her funding and mandating that she support productive engagement—was to change her stance. She didn't play into the drama. The leaders at other agencies did, and cut staff and property improvements. Some of those agencies wound up having to merge. Other agencies actually approached Vicki to ask her to absorb them into CBS. Vicki's response to the stars not aligning was to expand the boundaries of CBS's universe from home-based caregiving to a vertically integrated supply chain with diversified services and the birth of a new self-sustaining division, Good Reasons. The driver behind her brilliance, in addition to her great mind, was her integrity.

Integrity means standing strong for what you believe in, being honest about what you can and cannot do, and treating others with the same moral and value standards that you hold yourself to. It means that you can sleep at night because your highest self has risen to an occasion.

The Drink

CURVEBALL

2 ounces of gin
¼ teaspoon dry vermouth
¼ teaspoon triple sec
¼ teaspoon bitters
¼ teaspoon lemon juice
1 ounce whiskey
2 olives with pimiento

Blend the ingredients, topping the mixture with the whiskey and olives. Rim with integrity—owning what's yours. Howl at the moon.

Managing a curveball with integrity means you can look at whatever is coming, like a full blue moon and Mercury in retrograde, decide that it will be for the better, and then make it so. You transmute a potentially bad outcome to a positive one. It's a choice to take what is not expected and find an opportunity within it. Changing your stance, swinging a little differently, can transform a curveball from a foul ball into a base hit.

- Gin: its distinctive flavor comes from juniper berry and botanicals. Originally used as an herbal medicine in the Middle Ages, it became a commercial spirit. Medicine or cocktail, it's a matter of perspective.
- Dry vermouth: a fortified wine with wormwood and spices, it also went from medicine to cocktail.
- Triple sec: it adds a sweet orange flavor to bring in sweetness—always welcome when transmuting.

- Bitters: it also went from medicine to cocktail. It offers the combination of bittersweetness and aids in digestion, the helper in getting it all to work.
- Whiskey: distilled from grain, it has no medicinal background except as a general anesthetic when having a bullet removed. Good guys and bad guys alike drink it in the movies, so why not?
- Olives with pimiento: as in life, the sweet and sour are united and can work.
- Own what is yours: integrity to tell the truth makes even the strongest drinks go down smoothly, whether medicinal, cocktail, sweet, or sour.
- Howl at the moon—because it's there!

Here's to owning what's yours!

5

COMMUNICATION: What Did You (Not) Say?

JAMES BECAME A REGULAR after teaching Ian how to eat crabs. Then he taught the Five Guys from the neighborhood how to eat a steamed dozen, and they became fixtures at the Maryland Crab House, too. Bruno would paper the entire space at the end of the bar for them. I'd set them up with pitchers of beer and pop their favorite music into our speakers, and they'd spend hours talking work, baseball, and neighborhoods. They were friendly with the other regulars and, usually, welcoming to newcomers.

One night a new guy sat at the bar next to them. He asked the Five Guys if the hard-shells were any good. He was from the South and had grown up cracking them. The Five Guys assured him they were. New Guy ordered a dozen and a Maryland brew, which he was delighted we had on offer.

Bruno set him up and then came to the service end of the bar to have a word with me. "I don't have a good feeling about that guy," he said.

"You got a thing about southerners?" I asked, kidding.

"I wasn't even thinking about that. There's just something about the way his eyes are following you around the bar that I don't like."

"It comes with the job, Bruno."

I thought nothing of it. Bartenders are part of the show. Pat had always had men watching her every move. "You don't even notice it after a while," she had said. "Be pleasant and friendly but don't lead them on. You never want anyone to feel like you're playing favorites or that they should wait for you after the shift. And never date anyone where you work. Keep your relationships and roles clear." Pat's advice was gospel.

New Guy cracked his crabs, drank beer, and tried to engage the Five Guys in conversation. They talked about the American Museum of Natural History, Fleet Week, and which musical to see on Broadway. All reasonable conversation that then strayed into one and then two of the three things that Pat taught me never to talk about behind the bar.

"So, you all from New York?" asked New Guy, dipping his fingers in the rinsing bowl.

"Those two are originally from Boston. This fellow on my right is from New Jersey, and the one on my left is local. I'm from St. Paul," said one of the Five Guys. We referred to him as "the Minnesotan."

"Oh, so you're all bleeding hearts."

The Five Guys looked at one another, asking in their unspoken language, *Who the hell is this guy?*

The Minnesotan answered him. "That's an interesting way of viewing city people."

"Well, you northerners are all Democrats," New Guy said, downing his beer.

"St. Paul is actually in the Midwest," the Minnesotan said.

"Same difference," said New Guy. I overheard this as I was clearing his finger bowl. It was time for me to explain the community rule I'd learned from Pat.

"No sex, politics, or religion—" I said, but before I could finish New Guy interrupted me.

"The rules for our first date?" he said, laughing.

"The rules of the bar. We never talk about sex, politics, or religion—things that can get people who are enjoying a drink into a quick head of steam."

New Guy looked confused and asked, "Then what the hell do you talk about?"

"Baseball, business, music, and movies," I told him with a smile.

"I am not going to sit here and talk about the Yankees," he said. His voice was rising.

"Then choose from one of the other three categories," I said, trying to make light of the situation.

"What are we playing, *Jeopardy!*? I thought this was a bar."

New Guy was getting testy, and the Five Guys were getting edgy. Time to cool the situation down.

I asked Bruno to change the music to Waylon Jennings. He thought I was kidding. Ever since we'd become a crab house, Andrew would play nothing but Waylon Jennings, and we'd change the music whenever he left the bar. It was an inside joke with the regulars. But this time we needed Waylon.

"I'm a Ramblin' Man" filled the air. The Five Guys gave me a *You have to be shitting me* look. New Guy was delighted.

"Girl after my own heart." He drank his beer, and I thought the storm had passed. But then New Guy turned to the Five Guy from New York.

"Hey, any of you guys date her?" He was pointing at me.

New York Five Guy took a deep breath and turned to face him. "No one dates Helen. She's the bartender, like one of the guys," he said, as if everyone in the world knew this. New Guy was not from this world.

"I've dated many barmaids in my day. It comes with the job," said New Guy. That was obnoxious, and I wanted to set him straight.

"The best way to enjoy hanging out with my customers is not to date any of them," I said.

"Why, do you only like girls?" Beer foam hung to his long mustache as he asked this question to my chest. Bruno came a little closer. The Five Guys were on alert.

"Sir, I'll get your check ready," I said and walked over to the service end of the bar to fill drink orders from the dining room. Bruno followed.

"Let's get him out of here," Bruno said. I had never seen him so protective or determined before.

"I agree. Let me get these drink tickets filled and I'll check him out."

"He may not go quietly if you cut him off," Bruno said. He really looked concerned. I didn't want to give this idea any traction. I moved quickly to set up drinks at the service end. Meanwhile, New Guy kept running his mouth.

"Well, if she only likes girls, I can change her back. Once she's had me, she'll be begging for more." I couldn't believe what I was hearing, but with my back turned, the words were not relaying the full heat of the situation.

The Five Guys were seething. One Boston Five Guy's jaw was clenched so tight that his cheek was twitching. The Minnesotan was standing behind his bar stool. Two others were sitting stick straight and staring dead ahead. New York Five Guy was tapping his fingers on the bar, hard. New Guy saw he had hit a nerve and kept hitting it.

"You all must be a bunch of fags if you don't want to bed down the barmaid," he said.

"In this part of the world, we call them bartenders," New York Five Guy said, talking really slow, as if New Guy needed the time to understand.

"Well, where I come from we call them barmaids, and they earn their tips the old-fashioned way," he said, banging his fist into his open hand and leering at me. Bruno moved in closer. I was still filling drink orders, hoping he would just shut up. I still wasn't getting the gravity of New York Five Guy's finger rapping.

Bruno came back to me. "Get him out NOW!" he said, and then went back to his position behind New Guy.

I stopped filling drink orders and totaled New Guy's check. I intended to ask him to settle immediately. Even if it meant he'd leave without paying, I was willing to cover it just to get him out of there.

It was too late.

New Guy threw his last jab. "I'll just screw her later and then tell all of you assholes about it."

Just as I stood in front of them, check in hand, New York Five Guy picked up his beer mug and landed it square on top of New Guy's head. CRACK. Bruno was splattered with blood, glass flew across the floor, and New Guy hit the ground hard. New York Five Guy looked like he was ready to kick him while he was down.

"STOP! DONT MOVE," I said, my voice sharp. New York Five Guy felt it. I grabbed a bar rag, filled it with ice, and tossed it to Bruno.

"Help him onto that banquette. Get the hostess to sweep up the glass. I'm calling for an ambulance," I ordered.

This offer of assistance wasn't good enough for New Guy. Woozy but still able to run his mouth, he said, "I want that motherfucker arrested! He cracked my head open. I didn't touch him. I want you to call the cops. NOW!!!"

"Sir, I don't want to hear one more word out of your mouth. GET IT?" I gave him the "She crazy" look and he sat back. Later, Bruno told me that I also had the baseball bat that I kept hidden behind the bar in my hand.

**ADVICE: PAY ATTENTION. Communication
is more than just words.**

I glared at New York Five Guy. He was defending me, and he was
wrong. Maybe I should have been grateful that he cared so much, but
I was livid. He'd broken one of our community rules: No violence.
EVER. The year before, New York Five Guy had gotten into an argument with the Minnesotan's cousin. He stood up and started pushing
him. I got Bruno to step in between them and told New York Five Guy
that if he couldn't control his temper, he should drink in the meatpack-
ing district. He apologized and smoothed things over with the cousin,
and there had not been another incident. Until tonight.

In New York City, anytime you call an ambulance from a bar,
the police come with it. Since we were around the corner from a
hospital and the police academy, both would be there in minutes.
New York Five Guy got off his bar stool, his bleeding hand wrapped
in a napkin.

"Sit down," I said through clenched teeth. We glared at each other.

The Minnesotan appealed to me, saying, "He's got to get out of
here. This guy doesn't know anything about him. Come on, let's go
before the cops come."

"You. Can't. Leave," I said. I was stern and steady, my eyes locked with
his, my heart in my throat. I really liked the Five Guys. We had a history
together. They'd helped me show Andrew that I could build a bar scene. If
I didn't let New York Five Guy leave, they were not likely to return.

"Sit down, all of you. The police are going to want to take statements."

After I called for the ambulance, I called Andrew. He was at his
second restaurant, Steak Frites, which he had opened a few blocks away.
I told him there had been a bar fight and the police and an ambulance

were on their way. He asked if I was okay and said he would be right over.

Bruno got the place cleaned up. Marco kept control of the dining room while the ambulance and police carted off their respective subjects. Andrew stayed at the bar for the rest of the evening. Four of the Five Guys were sitting with him. I brought them all coffee.

"Why didn't you let him leave? This is going to cost him a fortune," the Minnesotan asked, distressed.

"Because he hit the guy over the head with his beer mug," I said. I tried not to be defensive, but I felt under attack.

"That guy was an asshole and deserved it and more," said New Jersey Five Guy indignantly. "He was really protecting you. If they charge him with felony assault, he can lose his brokerage license."

"But the guy never raised his hands. He just had a big mouth."

"A nasty mouth. Hey, Andrew, do you know what he was saying?" The Minnesotan filled Andrew in on the whole story. Andrew listened, shook his head, and said nothing.

New Jersey Five Guy was pointing his finger at me, asking why I would do this, especially since New Guy would never have been able to identify any of them. I tried to explain how I was honored that he wanted to stand up for me, but he had put us all at risk. He could have killed New Guy. New York Five Guy had created this mess, and he would have to deal with cleaning it and his temper up.

"Bullshit," New Jersey Five Guy said, his chin thrust forward. "The guy had it coming. What do you think, Andrew?"

"I wasn't here, so I can't say. But I do know that Helen did what she thought was best for everyone involved."

"You're a fucking politician, you know that?" New Jersey Five Guy said. He put down his coffee cup, and they all left.

Bruno, in his blood-spotted shirt, stayed until everyone was gone. Then he sat at the bar.

"Pour us all a shot of something," Andrew said. "And then come sit at this end with us." I mixed a Speak Easy and brought the shaker and three shot glasses with me.

Andrew was sitting in front of the banquette, facing both of us. I poured the shots. We drank and sat. Bruno broke the silence.

"The guy was an asshole, Andy. I didn't like him from the minute he sat down. He was staring at her, following her every move."

"Everybody stares at her. She's the bartender, she's good to look at, and she's entertaining," Andrew said.

"Yeah, but this guy was different. I can't explain it—more of a gut feeling. That's why I stayed close."

"Well, Bruno, your gut was right," Andrew said, pouring more of the shaker into our shot glasses. We downed them again.

I realized that I was shaking. After the police had come, I kept my cool and acted as if nothing unusual had happened. The bar buzzed with gossip, the dining room guests lingered longer than usual, but I was business as usual. However, now that it was over, I was filled with so much adrenaline that I couldn't sort it out. Andrew sat next to me and put his arm around me. More silence. I thanked Bruno for having my back. He offered to stay while we closed. Andrew thanked him, walked him to the door, and slipped him a bill to take a cab home.

Andrew came back to the stool near the banquette so we could talk face-to-face.

In as gentle a voice as I had ever heard him use, he asked, "If Bruno saw it coming, how come you didn't?"

"I knew the guy had stepped over the line. I was filling drink orders and stopped to get his check ready so I could get him out of here."

"So what happened?"

"I was listening to the banter but wasn't looking to see what was really going on."

"You know that New York Five Guy is a hothead. What were you thinking?" Andrew's voice was not accusatory. He was being mindful of how vulnerable I was feeling.

"I obviously didn't think he would cross the line. I trusted him." I put my head in my hands for a few moments and then sat up straight again.

"I'm sorry," I said. "I should have been paying better attention. I know that words can be bullshit and the face tells all." On the basketball court on Grand Street, people talked shit, but when you looked at them you could see they meant nothing by it.

"This could have been worse," Andrew said. "We got lucky. One more question. Why didn't you let New York Five Guy leave? This is going to really cost him."

"Because he broke the rules of the bar," I said.

"Come on, this isn't kindergarten. This is a guy and his career we are talking about."

"And you have this great business that you've worked hard to create. And we all have good jobs here. And the customers come here expecting great food and good service. They don't come here expecting brawling and police and ambulances." I drained the last drops out of the shaker into my shot glass.

"This community is about food and drink, not about blood and glass," I said. "I've been around blood and glass and don't want to be near it again." My Grand Street memories contributed to my trembling. We were a multiracial group of poor and working-class kids in a drug- and gang-infested area. Fistfights, stabbings, and overdoses were commonplace.

Andrew hailed a cab and rode downtown with me to my apartment. He asked the driver to wait and walked me to my door. I assured him that I was okay. He hugged me, said that I had done the right thing, then thanked me for watching his back and for caring. He waited until I was through the door and in the elevator before he got back in his cab.

Four months passed without our seeing hide nor hair of the Five Guys, until one night New York Five Guy came in by himself. He had just settled his case; it had cost him a small fortune, but he wouldn't lose his brokerage license.

"I'm sorry. I had to," I said.

"You were right. I have a short fuse. It sucked to go through that, but I learned my lesson."

On cue, the four others walked in and took seats at the bar. I started to say something, but the Minnesotan held up his hand to stop me. He asked for five dozen hard-shells and a pitcher of beer. I motioned for Bruno to set up the bar.

Leadership Is More Than Management

Communication is so much more than language. Its universe includes choice of terms, expressions, emotions, body language, and instinct. It can convey intended and unintended messages. Words can say one thing, but tone of voice and how one holds one's arms and tilts one's head can convey something very different.

Because communication is multifaceted, people send and receive messages that are both deliberate and unintentional, conscious and unconscious. A sender chooses to speak face-to-face and to be loud, soft, or silent. The person on the receiving end interprets the message through their own experiences, perceptions, mood, and personality. Interpretation creates meaning.

Leaders and managers need to be astute communicators. There's a saying: "You should communicate with two ears and one mouth." I would add: "And listen to your intuition." Communication has context; it is more than listening. It is also observing and feeling the current in the air, interpreting the message being sent in the setting where it is transmitted.

Paying attention takes effort. Don't assume that you already know what another person is going to say or do. Don't finish others' sentences before they have a chance to speak their minds.

Sometimes communication is revealed by action. New York Five Guy communicated that he cared about me and that he was a hothead. But sometimes the most important message is revealed through inaction. If you don't know much about people, notice how they dress, groom themselves, hold their bodies, and whether they look you in the eye when they speak. If you are in someone's office or home, notice the books on the bookshelf, their collectibles, how they use space. You can pick up cues about people just by paying attention.

After the Bar

Inaction May Be Just a Prelude to Action

The CEO of a well-respected global marketing and advertising conglomerate wanted to cross-sell more services across its vast network of companies: he wanted to "keep the money in the family." I had worked with this CEO before when I was subcontracted to bring a strategic and intelligence perspective on a different project. He appreciated my dual focus—business strategy and behavioral science—and preferred to work with me on projects in need of both the art and science of change.

My mission was to guide a group of senior managers to design a new, cooperative way of conducting business. Instead of engaging agencies outside the internal network in client projects, incentives would be created to leverage their sister agencies' skills. So part of the new way of doing business was to also create incentives for keeping more business inside the "family."

The senior managers represented two different brands ("Big Brand" and "Brand Two") across distinct areas of expertise such as market research, public relations, creative direct-to-consumer advertising, promotion, and media services. Big Brand represented a higher percentage of billable hours than did Brand Two. In both, the players were very bright and very political. Some were also very high-maintenance. Each was convinced their role, perspective, creativity, and know-how were essential for successfully winning and maintaining big clients. In short, they felt entitled.

It would have been easier working with Hollywood starlets. One vice president sent her assistant to her apartment-building doorman every morning to pick up her briefcase because she liked to walk to work and didn't want to carry anything. She would also drink only Evian. Another demanded absolute silence while she talked. One media buyer claimed to have "discovered" the series *Survivor*; what he had actually done was buy a large share of advertising airtime before the show became a hit. The way he talked about it, you would have thought he was the show's actual executive producer. Media buyers get to see previews of upcoming network-television shows at a yearly gathering called the Up-Fronts. They then purchase advertising time slots for specific clients or to have in their portfolios to make available to clients during the season.

My job was to get them to play nice, share their toys, and collaboratively come up with a new system for selling to and servicing clients. My saving grace here was the finish line: each senior manager would get his or her moment of fame by participating in a presentation of the group's recommendations to the presidents of all the conglomerate's companies. This was an opportunity for all of them to be noticed by the company's highest-level decision makers, who were otherwise hard to get an audience with.

The group agreed that they should use each other's services more and "keep the money in the family"—flowing among them instead of outside to competing companies—as the CEO had requested. Big Brand thought that consolidating their efforts would be more efficient and make them more competitive. Big Brand wanted to restructure and collapse the two brands into one: theirs.

I explained how different structures could work, highlighting the pros and cons of one- and two-brand solutions. To my surprise, once the Brand Two people understood that their jobs would be secure and their bonuses might increase with more internal money flow, they began to agree with the Big Brand people. Working with this new structure, they readily created informal and formal systems for more efficient client and creative management.

In my consulting career, I learned early never to waste an executive's time when I didn't have an answer, and never to surprise the person in charge. So I sent the CEO weekly "view from the trenches" e-mails. To convey the news that the team wanted to restructure, I requested that we meet days before the big presentation. I was surprised that Brand Two was considering collapsing their resources under the umbrella of Big Brand, and I didn't know where the CEO stood on this or how he would respond. He, too, was surprised by the one-brand solution, as he had not anticipated that Brand Two would want to consolidate. He wanted to see how this scenario played out at the meeting and was fine with our moving ahead on the presentation to all the presidents. At the presentation, the presidents of Big Brand and Brand Two would be hearing of the plan for the first time.

At the big meeting, the group seamlessly moved from function to brand and presented the "client service model" of the future. They talked about more collaboration early in the process, streamlining work flow, and engaging multiple perspectives. They did not indicate that this was a one-brand platform until their closing comments.

When they finally revealed the new structure, the president of Brand Two, who would be out of a job if this restructuring took place, was very quiet and maintained a poker face. During Q & A, he said nothing. At the conclusion, the CEO asked the Brand Two president to comment. The group braced themselves, because the Brand Two president was known as a scrapper, but he calmly admitted that he was surprised and would like to think about it some. He thought the systems were quite good. Perhaps they could meet at the same time next week to discuss more of the details. The CEO then asked the group to provide data that would support merging their brands and pooling their structural efficiencies.

The group took the Brand Two president's response as a victory, but I warned them that scrappers don't go down easily and that they should prepare for a strong response. I was more nervous by what he wasn't communicating than by what he was. The group believed that what they had presented made so much sense that the more the Brand Two president thought about it, the more he would relent. Hubris is the enemy of reading a situation the right way. I left the meeting and headed straight for a Speak Easy cocktail.

The next week the group, presidents, CEO, and I all reconvened. The group presented their data. Then, without having a slot on the agenda, the president of Brand Two stepped to the podium and opened a presentation of his own. I held my breath. I caught the eye of the CEO. Apparently he had been expecting a full-out attack on the one-brand plan. And it was masterful.

The Brand Two president dissected the group's plan point by point, refuting their data with his own. He drew blood. He demonstrated that although his company didn't bill as many actual dollars, the profit margins were more robust. He also demonstrated that his firm had attracted more new clients in the past three years, while Big Brand's sales growth relied on a few large existing accounts—a lot of eggs in too few baskets. He pushed his sword in deeper when he capped his argument by financially demonstrating that Brand Two's new clients came from growth industries, whereas Big Brand was relying on legacy industries. Based on this data and his intimation that Big Brand might not be bigger for long, he agreed with the one-brand mode—his—and that he should run the merger of the two. He already knew how to drive efficiency and effectiveness in a complex organization. He cited his experience as both COO and CFO before becoming president and the extended connections he had woven over his multidecade career.

This ignited the president of Big Brand, and the arrows flew. The group sat stunned. The scrapper Brand Two president's quiet response the week before had been calculated, a weapon of a warrior under attack.

The CEO let the battle rage until no new information was being shared, then took the helm. He had decided from the start that the two brands would remain separate, and for a simple and sound reason: two brands create double the opportunity to win RFPs (requests for pro-posals). He also thought that a little internal competition kept every-one on their toes. He lauded the collaborative systems that the team created and adopted the plan in full—to serve two brands, not one.

The president of Brand Two thanked the group. The other execu-tives filtered out of the room and also congratulated the group. Mem-bers of the group were too numb from their perceived loss to realize that they had really won. They were recognized by their executives as assertive, bright stars who could craft a new business model. They learned, albeit the hard way, how to expand their business acumen.

And they also received a serving of humility, an important ingredient for successful communication.

———

Communication is about creating meaning. This is not easy. You need to stay awake and pay attention. It means not multitasking when the message matters, not reading e-mail while talking on the phone. It does mean multisensing: reading all the cues available when engaging with someone.

Communication can be tangible or intangible. Tangible communication is easy: words and actions match. It is easy to attribute meaning when a person does what she says she will. Andrew thanked me for caring about him and the restaurant (tangible), and his actions and sympathy communicated that he cared about me and understood that in the moment I was vulnerable. He wanted me to know he was there for me (intangible). That simple act of accompanying me home in the taxi communicated what really mattered.

Intangible communication is more complex, more open to interpretation. Just because someone says something doesn't mean you know what that person will do. New Guy never had a chance of hooking up with me. New York Five Guy interpreted his words as an intention to do so and reacted, although he could have made other choices that would have communicated his protectiveness. For instance, he could have stayed to make sure I didn't close the bar alone. The opposite is also true. Just because someone says nothing doesn't mean that he will do nothing. The president of Brand Two said little but a week later came out swinging. If the group had paid more attention to his history and experience, they might not have celebrated so early. But if they had given too much consideration to his reputation, they might not have come up with a single-brand solution at all. His reputation might have intimidated them enough to keep them from thinking outside the box after they agreed to a one-brand solution. They might have been more caught up in circumnavigating his ire than in attending to the mission they were brought together to achieve.

It's important to learn about the people you work with. It contributes to understanding how and what they communicate. However, that knowledge should be a guidepost and not a roadblock. Knowing about a person's possible response to a situation can be taken into account as *a* thing to have in the mix and not *the* thing. That's how you create a balance between knowledge as a facilitator of action and knowledge as a showstopper.

The Drink

SPEAK EASY

2 tablespoons of St-Germain

3.5 ounces prosecco

1 teaspoon of Chambord

1 sprig of rosemary

Blend the ingredients, soaking the rosemary in the mixture. Infuse with active attention, muddle in the rules of the playground, stir, then serve over ice.

Successful communication demands that both the sender and receiver engage in active attention. You need to be determined to create understanding, to share the vision of an intended message. You need to practice mindfulness and aim to interpret a message with integrity and honesty. Combining these ingredients to create meaning is at the heart of leadership. Being awake means that all of our senses, even the elusive sixth sense, are engaged. And this needs to happen seamlessly for purpose and understanding to be in concert.

In a Speak Easy, the intended communication is joy: fruitful, aromatic, not too sweet, sparkling, and woody. The bartender has to mix it with balance and patience, and be mindful of presentation. To experience it fully, the taster should first notice its color, then catch its scent, sip, and experience the light effervescence and taste the flowers and wood, feeling refreshed, like walking through a meadow at the end of a wooded trail.

- St-Germain: made from elderflowers, it is very aromatic, with many undertones. Devote some time to capture its full essence.
- Prosecco: a sparkling wine best imbibed early, before the bubbles flatten.
- Chambord: although made from black raspberry, this is a very complex liqueur, a reminder not to be lured into a false sense of security when something seems sweet.
- Rosemary: a woody perennial that is thought to enhance cognitive function and memory, a reminder to stay awake.
- Community sense: the rules of the playground. Look the person in the eye and remember who they are before responding.
- Active attention: select and focus on what is important.

Here's to knowing whom you are dealing with and being able to duck quickly!

EMPATHY: Love Your Barback

EARLY IN MY CINCINNATI tenure, before the staff became a crew that trusted one another, I was an outsider. The first week I worked, the staff was helpful in getting me schooled in the menu and their way of doing things. But by the third week Marco became very snippy. His behavior set an example for the rest of the staff, who all became more demanding and less patient, huffing and pounding their hands on the service bar, rolling their eyes because they had to wait. I would make eye contact with them to let them know that I was there, but I did not react to their attitude. Still, they carried on.

At the end of my shifts, I was exhausted. Bruno still ran plates to the bar's customers who ordered food, but he did not act as barback. He would not bring the dish rack or restock the bar. I kept the wait-staff's orders moving, but they were stingy on the tip out and left without saying good night. I needed to figure out what the story was if I was going to make Cincinnati my nirvana, my home. I decided to have dinner there on my night off. I thought this would give me a greater understanding of their reality and get to know them a little better.

Marco was livid when he saw me seated in his section. "What the hell do you think you're doing here?" he asked.

I told him I wanted to experience the dining room so I could serve them better.

"Are you going to take out your little pad and take notes, too?"

His vitriol took me by surprise, but I smiled and said, "Great idea."

"Bullshit. First, Andrew doesn't hire women bartenders, but then he hires you. Okay, fine, you do a good job. But now he comes in less to check up on things. There can only be one reason for that: you're spying on us and reporting back."

The staff's hostility now made some sense. Because I was part of a change, I was suspect. They were nervous, thinking that if Andrew did this one thing differently—hiring me—and it worked, then he would also do other things differently . . . and they liked things the way they were. In fact, Andrew had stopped coming in as often because I was better at running the bar than his other bartender. They thought the whole thing was a setup, including my coming in for dinner. I needed to figure out how to create a comfort zone, to reassure the staff that I was part of "Us" and not "Them."

I asked Marco if he would like me to leave. He said yes. I stood up and pushed my chair away from the table. He looked surprised. He had expected an argument.

"I came in tonight because I know the staff has an issue with me. I wanted you to get to know me better. Now I understand why you could be suspicious. But I'm just a girl trying to pay my rent. Can I come back after the shift and take you out for a drink?"

Marco paused, and then he motioned for me to sit back down. He handed me a menu.

"Order the she-crab soup, and I'll bring a tasting of what's popular."

Two days later, when I arrived for my shift, the hostess greeted me as I walked through the door. Marco came over with the specials and explained them without any of his usual irritation. The others waved. I had turned the corner with the waitstaff.

But not with Bruno. He used to restock the bar after lunch, before my shift. Apparently he didn't have time anymore, because now he "needed to fold napkins." I was last on his to-do list.

Marco had told me that Bruno never thought I was a spy. His cold shoulder was from something else. But without Bruno's help, I wouldn't be able to provide the tight service that I wanted to—not for the customers, who were more forgiving, or the waitstaff, who didn't know the word "forgiving." I could be only as good as the people who supported me.

I needed to figure out his story. In the meantime I went down to the basement and brought up what I needed to get through the night.

––––––––––

Before I became a bartender, I waitressed at a small restaurant called Singer's in Liberty, New York, in the Catskill Mountains. There you could get a five-course meal for $5.95 from a full American, Chinese, and deli menu. At any time a single table could demand an eleven-condiment setup: duck sauce, hot mustard, soy sauce, ketchup, deli mustard, Russian dressing, mayonnaise, steak sauce, pickles, rolls, and Chinese noodles. Efficiency was impossible. It was rare that a table of four would place a drink, side, or dessert order at the same time. That meant a lot of running around.

At Singer's I learned that the busboy, like a barback, is essential for good service. If the busboy gets rolls and water to a table right away, people are more patient about placing their orders when the floor is busy. The busboy makes sure that there's clean silverware and removes used plates to make room for the next course. He cleans up what the servers drop and sometimes helps carry things when their hands are full. He is their support, their backbone.

Eduardo, our busboy at Singer's, didn't speak much English but understood what we needed. In his early twenties, with thick brown hair, he never smiled or frowned, was constantly in motion, and never commented on how we tipped him at the end of the night.

Eduardo tended to pay more attention to the senior waitresses because they were irritable and bossy. I could get him to clear the table, but I was often on my own with rolls and water. I couldn't talk to him about this because I didn't speak Spanish. The senior waitresses liked this arrangement and did nothing to change it. The owner, fearful of these waitresses, wasn't willing to address it, either.

At the end of one grueling Sunday shift, I was so hot and tired that my eyelashes hurt. Through the kitchen and out the back door was a wide alleyway with a couple of chairs. I stepped out to catch my breath. I opened the door slowly and heard music. Classical guitar. Quietly, I closed the door behind me and took a few steps closer to see who it was.

Eduardo was strumming and picking an old guitar, making impossibly beautiful music. In his stained white shirt and greasy tennis shoes, his eyes closed, he was in concert, oblivious to me, the stars, and the smell of frying oil. I stood there in silence. There was something mournful about his playing. It seemed to come from someplace beyond the alley, beyond Singer's, beyond Liberty. I left quietly.

I asked Felipe, the nicer cook, about Eduardo the next day. In Guatemala, where Eduardo was from, he had studied music at their best school and had a growing reputation in his province. During one of the coups, his older brother was arrested for sympathizing with the opposition. Fearing that Eduardo would be next, his mother sold her valuables and had him smuggled to the United States. All he had now was his guitar, the memory of his family, and this demanding, dirty, and thankless job. He worked as many shifts as many days a week as he could so that he could bring his mother, whom he hadn't seen in two years, to the United States.

I was in awe. This young man had already lost more than I had ever gained. Every shift he showed up trying to do what he thought was best, for a purpose bigger than I could have ever imagined. At this point in my life, freedom was the ability to buy things for myself with my own money. Freedom for Eduardo was freedom from harm and the ability to play his guitar—anywhere. Knowing Eduardo's story changed how I saw him, as a busboy and as a person. It made me feel a little more grateful for my own station in the world.

The next time I was at the local record store, I bought a classical guitar album. I wrapped it in newspaper and wrote on it, in Spanish, *Salud!* Felipe, the cook, saw me come into the kitchen with the package. I told him that I had a present for Eduardo. He suggested that I not give it to him because he didn't have a record player. It never occurred to me that Eduardo wouldn't have a record player.

The next day I found an old record player buried in a mess of posters, books, and rugs in the back room of the Liberty Craft Store across the street from Singer's. The owner, Walter, often came in at the end of my shift for a corned-beef sandwich. He was a fiftysomething in a tie-dyed shirt, love beads, and a white guy's Afro, the town poet who taught classes at the community college in the winter. The store always smelled like a mix of sandalwood and mold, incense and history, rolled into a small space that needed a paint job, a roof, and more customers. I told Walter Eduardo's story and why the record player was for him.

"I've wondered where that music came from. I hear it some nights when I leave Singer's. It's so out of place in the alleyway." Walter plugged in the record player and the turntable turned. He offered to clean it up and find a new needle.

A week later the record player was ready. Walter came in at the end of my shift. We walked around Singer's to the back alleyway. Felipe was there, and the three of us sat on an empty drum of cooking oil and listened to Eduardo play. After Felipe bid us good night, Walter and I gave Eduardo our gift. Eduardo's eyes opened wide and then he shook his head no. Walter spoke to him in Spanish. He told him that we wanted to hear him play more often. The record player would increase his selection. Understanding that Eduardo was proud, instead of a gift, Walter made a trade. Eduardo would accept the record player and we would meet on Tuesday and Thursday nights, after hours, behind the restaurant for a concert.

The next day at work, Eduardo was different, a bit lighter in his step. After a few weeks of sitting in the greasy alley, Walter moved our concert to his store. Soon people began gathering outside the window to listen, so he decided to open the store and let people in. Walter put a hat in front of Eduardo with some coins in it. The listeners would add to the coins and sometimes buy something from the store. I got to listen to beautiful music in a town whose jukeboxes were stuck on borscht-belt favorites like Paul Anka and Steve & Eydie. And I got rolls on the table, I didn't have to fight for silverware, and we all made more money for the rest of the summer. We all had gotten what we needed. Everyone has a story.

ADVICE: Care enough to discover the story and uncover a key to win-win.

Back at Cincinnati, we were getting slammed and I was buried. Andrew came in and was surprised to see glasses piling up and a near-empty condiment tray.

"Where's Bruno?"

I said he was busy in the dining room and that I needed to prepare better for Friday night. I could tell Andrew didn't buy this.

That night, after closing, Andrew sat at the bar.

"I've been thinking about Bruno, why he left you in the lurch. I should have known this would happen."

A few days before I had come in asking for a job, Bruno himself had asked for a chance to tend bar. Andrew had told him that if he didn't find someone with experience in the next week, he would consider letting Bruno shadow a quiet shift with the other bartender. Then I was hired, and as I picked up more shifts, Andrew never created the opportunity for Bruno.

In Bruno's mind, I was the spoiler. I had displaced him, taken away his chance to work his way out of the kitchen to behind the bar. I could relate; I had been there.

I offered to start teaching Bruno the basics, just as Pat had taught me. Andrew was opening for brunch in a couple of months. We could offer Bruno a shift. At first Andrew balked, wanting to keep Bruno in the dining room, because he was so good at it. But I was concerned that if we didn't provide him with the opportunity, he would leave. My plan was to keep him in both places for as long as we could. It also provided us depth on the bench: another bartender to fill in when someone got sick or quit.

The next time I saw Bruno, I asked him in front of Andrew to come in thirty minutes earlier for my next shift. He was annoyed and cast a pleading look at Andrew. Andrew shrugged. I pushed.

"Come on, Bruno, I'll be coming in early, too." I didn't want to share with Bruno what Andrew and I were planning just then. I wanted to tell him when we were alone, in case his distaste for me was because of something other than what Andrew and I had thought. It would give me the opportunity to try to work things out with him.

Andrew was watching, so Bruno finally said, "Sure."

When I arrived for my shift at 3:30 p.m. the next day, Bruno was already sitting at the bar.

"What do you want?" His tone was caustic.

I walked behind the bar and put on my apron. "Put this on." I gave him one.

"Bullshit." He put it on the bar.

I took out my paring knife and cutting board, as well as lemons, limes, oranges, and the condiment tray. I handed him a small cutting board and a paring knife.

"Why am I here?"

"You're going to learn how to cut twists and slices. It looks easier than it is. I'm going to show you how to make them all the same size." I was channeling my inner Pat. She had told me if I was going to invest my time in something, I should do it right.

"I'm not doing your work for you. This is bullshit." He started for the door.

"You're going to need to know how to do this when we open for brunch next month. Saturday is your shift. Unless of course you'll be too tired from the Friday dinner push."

He stopped walking and turned around.

"What are you talking about?" he asked.

I shared the discussion I had had with Andrew. Bruno put on his apron.

"Why are you doing this for me?"

"I've been in your shoes. I know how it feels when you have to get out of the kitchen. I was lucky to have someone teach me. It's my turn to pass it on."

"What's it going to cost me?" he asked. He seemed really confused by my offer, as if being given something without a price tag was a novel experience. I had learned how to trade from Walter.

"You're smart, you work hard, and you want to learn. We all do better when we help each other be our best. I'm better at what I do with your help. You'll understand how much I respect what you do when you're running your own bar. Now, wash your hands and let's get going."

Bruno washed his hands and started mangling a lemon. Before long, I started my shift with enough condiments and mixes to get through a busy night. At first Bruno and I restocked the bar together. Later he started doing it for me. The glass rack reappeared. He got his brunch shift the next month. And all was well in Cincinnati.

Leadership Is More Than Management

Business is about trading, exchanging know-how for payment. Good management clarifies workers' roles, matches each person's ability to the needs of each job, and then compensates fairly for the exchange. Leadership leaps beyond task fulfillment. It nurtures people, fulfilling the vision they have for themselves. The leader facilitates opportunity and growth, and the employee invests the best of his or her talents. This is a good trade, a win-win.

Eduardo and Bruno were being managed but not led. They knew what was expected of them, had the skills to fulfill those expectations, and were paid for performing their duties. By giving Bruno a chance to learn a new skill and make more money, Andrew ensured that he stayed. Cincinnati benefited by keeping an excellent barback who could also manage the difficult dining room crew and now fill another role as well.

The exchange with Eduardo at Singer's had been of a different sort. I not only got rolls for my tables and enjoyed his beautiful music but, once I knew about all that Eduardo had sacrificed, his job was elevated, and I was more generous in my tip out at the end of the night. I wanted Eduardo to transcend the dirty dishes and water pitchers that defined his life. I was rooting for him to succeed as he was able to play for a wider audience.

Empathy is at the heart of leadership. Organizations have character, purpose, and attitudes of their own, but they are still composed of people, who have their own personalities, drive, and stories. It is easier to get lost in the soul of an organization than to become familiar with the diverse individuals that make it tick, but people enable organizations to do what they do. It is worth the effort to get to know people.

After the Bar

Give Without the Ask

The School of Management at Marist College has thirty-four full-time professors, no one really knows how many adjuncts, one associate dean, two assistant deans, one dean, a handful of student elves, and four administrative-support people for approximately one thousand undergraduate business majors and five hundred MBA and MPA graduate students.

The challenge here is not in managing the students but in managing the full-time faculty. The saying "It's like herding cats" could be about our senior faculty. I have had the privilege of this title—professor and cat—for nearly three decades, with more than twenty of those years in the School of Management at Marist College.

Our faculty is an impossible and talented gaggle of people who put students first and all else second. We do not have graduate assistants to help us with research, so we rely on the student elves and our administrative support to manage our sundry needs, reasonable and not. And they manage us, for the most part with efficiency and good humor.

One day I was in the dean's office talking about staffing for a special degree program, when I heard someone speaking impeccable French. We professors are happy when we get students to speak clear English without the "like," "you know," and "I mean" ticks, so the beautiful French was a surprise. When I walked into the reception area to see who this talent was, I was surprised to find Renee, our thirtysomething, bright-eyed, pixie-haired secretary, on the phone speaking in a perfect accent and rhythm.

I was staring, so she put her conversation on hold, and asked, "You okay, Professor Rothberg? Do you need me for something?"

"No, but who are you talking to?"

"Jean-Claude. He's an adjunct teaching marketing for us."

"In French?"

Renee laughed. "No, of course not. I don't get the opportunity to practice often, so we always speak in French," Renee said, matter-of-factly, as if everyone were bilingual.

This wasn't Renee's only remarkable attribute. The first time I sent her a student recommendation to print on stationery, she asked if it was okay for her to edit it before I signed the final copy, and she improved it in several ways. She can also fix the copy machine and printers, find classroom space when all of it is booked, manage catering for special events, and get seventy-five binder clips on a moment's notice. She could probably change the fluid in my transmission. And she does it all with an even temper, a smile, and a "Yes" even when she is swamped. And she doesn't do this just for me—she does it for ALL of us cats.

Why is Renee our support person when she can run the place? What's her story?

Renee decided early on that her most important job was raising her children. She worked in a nursery school for ten years, which is actually very good training for managing faculty. Renee now works for us because Marist College has a magnificent policy where any child of any employee, if smart enough to get accepted, can attend the college for free. And, like their mother, her children are smart.

During the holiday season and on Administrative Assistant Day, two or three of us try to round up the herd and weasel money out of them to buy our support staff tokens of our gratitude. This takes about two weeks. We're lucky to get $350. I think one time we actually shook them down for $400. It's not that the faculty is unappreciative; they're just hard to corner and tend not to carry cash. We always sign the card collectively "From the Third Floor."

Renee rarely missed a day in the office. And then she did—a lot— and some of us started asking why. We discovered that she would be gone for at least one month (without pay for almost all of it) because her husband had been diagnosed with stage four colon cancer. She was with him for his surgery and recovery, her sister-in-law helping with her children. That time it was easy to create a collection for Renee. In less than three days the faculty and dean collected more than $4,000. Renee was shocked, overwhelmed, and relieved. We didn't know at the time that her checking account that day was overdrawn by $112.

The faculty, for a moment, had realized that, whatever their own quotidian emergencies might have been—tests needing to be copied, travel budgets needing approval, a conference deadline—none of it mattered all that much. What mattered was that we cared enough to actually help someone who always helped us. We were relieved and nearly giddy when Renee returned. She didn't stay away long, wanting to come back to the insanity of us, a relief from the new normal of her life.

Renee's plight brought out our empathy and community, which shifted Renee's commitment to us. Over the next couple of years she took on progressively higher-level administrative duties. To our joy, she ultimately ascended to become the chief administrator of the School of Management.

Through her husband's protracted illness, Renee was stoic. When asked how he was doing, she always responded with a level "We are hanging in there." She was the Derek Jeter of academia, an example of professionalism and grace to all of us. My appreciation of Renee as an incredible administrator expanded to include respect for her as an impressive person. My exchanges with her now extend beyond a cheerful thank-you. I try to contribute, to give back levity, in exchange for all she gives me. So I bring chocolate truffles on some days, silly cow-headed pens, or ginger hand cream and take her out for a bite or amuse her with some silly story. Our support of each other, in our own ways, makes us both better. Win-win.

Renee, Bruno, and Eduardo had skill sets that made their organizations tick. They could herd the cats, managing the varied personalities and expectations of the people they worked with. And they did so quietly and efficiently, asking for nothing in return but their paycheck or tips. Yet beneath their competent exteriors were personal stories that drove them to excel regardless of their ranks in the organizations or the roles that they played. Without them, none of the organizations would have performed as well. And our display of empathy for who they were, their stories, and their needs, and being able to offer each a gesture of recognition, elevated us individually and collectively.

Empathy is essential for building community and grounding an organization and its people. Leaders are the embodiment of their organizations. Their choice to act, and the type of action taken, demonstrates what they care about. And when such choices are made with integrity, the entire community benefits.

If we achieve our best because we have the support we need, then we should willingly give support to those we rely on. Sometimes support means money, sometimes it means time off. Sometimes it means hiring an extra person; sometimes it means providing training and new opportunity. Sometimes it means just saying thank you. And sometimes it means doing something out of the ordinary that makes that person feel visible and a valued part of the whole.

The Drink

PINK MARTINI

3 ounces vodka

1 ounce Alizé Red Passion

1 orange slice

Blend the vodka and Alizé Red Passion. Shake over ice, then strain into a martini glass. Squeeze orange slice in it. Rim with compassion. Add a dash of positive regard. Let settle.

Empathizing with someone's circumstances, caring about somebody's engagement in the community that makes up an organization, can have a large return. Empathy can take the sting out of difficult times, help people face tough challenges, and give them hope that their dreams can live on.

- Vodka: a solid yet flexible base that can take on many different mixers or stand alone, it can sting, and it can be smooth.
- Alizé Red Passion: a liqueur made from an evergreen superfruit with phytochemicals that may benefit the cardiovascular system with an anticlotting (clogging) agent. When blended with all martini ingredients, it renders the drink pink, the color of nurturing.
- Shaking over ice and straining: alter the temperature but not the potency.
- Orange slice: it blends (all) senses.
- Rimming with compassion: everyone has a story whose flavor can enhance the drink.
- A dash of positive regard: acceptance and support add balance.

Here's to daring to care!

ADVICE FOR LEADERSHIP

ADVICE: Standing in Your Own Shoes

I WAS IN MY fifth year in the City University of New York's doctoral program and had passed my comprehensive exams in organization and policy studies. I was now trying to get a third dissertation proposal accepted by the doctoral committee: Professor Menlo, the director of the PhD program; Professor Higgins, the director of the management major; and Professor Adams, a rising star on the graduate faculty.

Professor Higgins was my "rabbi," the guy I had persuaded to let me into the PhD program four years earlier, about a year after I had nudged my way into bartending at Cincinnati. I had wanted out of the MBA program and into a PhD, and decided to make my way into Professor Higgins's office to persuade him to admit me. I had just been to a dance class and was still in a leotard, leg warmers, and a wrap skirt, but instead of heading to the bar to get ready for my shift, I turned north and walked up Park Avenue South. I was thinking about the production and operations paper I had due on using queuing theory to calculate how to make a line in a bank move faster. I would rather have poked out my eye than spend the weekend on that. So I decided to try to see Higgins, who would be in his office because he was scheduled to teach in an hour.

I needed to persuade Professor Higgins to give me a chance because my liberal arts undergraduate degree didn't give me the qualifications to get into the program for a PhD in business. My only business education was the twelve MBA credits I had under my belt, three of which were for an elective in industrial organizational psychology: the scientific study of human behavior in the workplace. The business-foundation courses that I had to take for the MBA were foreign, and I was looking at three more semesters of them. When I'd looked at the requirements in the catalog, it seemed that I could earn the MBA while in the PhD program, and those credits would apply for both.

I foolishly thought that the PhD would involve just one more really big paper. I couldn't have been more wrong. Whereas bartending is one part drink pouring, one part creating a rhythm, one part psychology, and two parts control—the easy part is making the drinks, while the other parts require more finesse—getting a PhD required one part intelligence, one part luck in getting a thesis advisor, and two parts persistence and humility. The easy part is the learning. I had to work on all the other parts.

Professor Higgins's gatekeeper was a woman of fifty-five in a smart suit and short haircut. "You don't have an appointment and don't seem"—the secretary cleared her throat—"*ready* to meet with the program director." She eyed my outfit, obviously not approving of my striped leg warmers, burgundy leotard, and matching wrap skirt. She informed me that Professor Higgins never accommodated a drop-in and was very busy. When she looked down at the calendar to schedule me for some future date, I darted past her and into his office.

Professor Higgins was sitting in his big leather chair, the shades drawn, fast asleep. I took advantage and quickly looked around the office. I wanted to get a sense of whom I would be convincing. His office was a mess. Papers, books, pens, empty cups of coffee, folders, files, paper clips, rubber bands, and candy-bar wrappers were scattered everywhere. There were an outdated picture of his family and his framed degrees. His PhD was in psychology. His bookshelf was a jumble of organizational behavior and management journals. I stepped closer to his desk.

"Excuse me, Professor Higgins."

He startled awake.

"I'm Helen Rothberg." I extended my hand. He stared at me in disbelief. *NO ONE EVER* walked in on Professor Higgins, but he slowly lifted his hand and I shook it with an enthusiasm he wasn't ready for. His secretary was right behind me.

"Did we have an appointment?" he asked as he moved things around on his desk, looking for an appointment book that probably didn't exist. He glared at his secretary, who was about to speak, when I quickly explained that I had walked past her and in through his open door. He shook his head. I sensed that he was about to throw me out, so I threw my elbows.

"I'm currently enrolled in an MBA program. I'm bored to tears. There's got to be more to life than debits and credits and queuing theory. I've taken organizational behavior and loved it. I noticed that your program has a focus in this area. I'm very creative and believe your program would benefit from someone like me, someone who has a different perspective than a traditional graduate student in business."

NO ONE EVER told Professor Higgins what he should do. I kept talking.

He put his hand up for me to stop, then asked me a few questions. When he learned that my undergraduate focus was premed and then psychology, that I had never had a business course until the MBA program, and that I was just finishing my first year, he said, "You are not qualified to enter a PhD program in business, Ms. Rothberg. You don't have an MBA or any graduate degree, for that matter. You don't even have the fundamental business courses. Come back when you grow up, untangle your hair, and learn how to dress properly."

I threw another elbow and drove down the lane. I said that his program needed someone with a liberal arts background, like him, who thought out of the box. He was getting increasingly annoyed. First, I'd interrupted his nap, now I was arguing with him. He threatened to have me removed from the building. I proposed that I take whichever two MBA courses he suggested and two courses from the PhD program next fall. If I did well in the PhD courses, then I would be admitted to the program in the spring and earn the MBA en route.

"You have nothing to lose," I said.

I was employing the same tactic I had used to get a job at Cincinnati, offering to show my chops before asking for a commitment.

Professor Higgins turned his back to me in his swivel chair and looked toward the window with the shades drawn. He told me to register for his introductory course and Professor Menlo's introductory course, to take whatever MBA courses I wanted, and to get out of his office.

My scheme had worked, and I was accepted into the program. But over the next four years, Higgins didn't become any nicer, and now he had just rejected my second dissertation proposal: he wasn't interested in the topic. I was still working on a third revision, so I was surprised when I was summoned to Professor Higgins's office. Once a semester he called me into his office to tell me what I was doing that he didn't like. Sometimes he objected to my choice of elective, sometimes to where I was traveling during the summer. Today it was about where I was employed.

"Rothberg, you can't be a doctoral candidate and work at a bar. You need to be a research assistant if you ever hope to graduate. How are you going to learn anything about management and leadership if you are slinging gin instead of analyzing surveys and running regression analysis? What do you expect me to say about you during the doctoral-candidate review committee later today?"

After my meeting with Higgins, his dislike of my bartending job rented space in my brain. At the bar the chef was out sick, which meant that Andrew would be in the kitchen. This was not news I wanted to hear. First my mentor tells me I have to quit bartending. Now I find out that Andrew would be making everyone crazy. An excellent chef, he was meticulous and cranky about how the plates went out.

"Maybe it's a good thing I'm cooking," Andrew said. "I got a tip that we might be getting reviewed tonight." He was trying to arrange the financing for another restaurant. A good review would validate his talent and bolster his chances.

"Great," I said, but I sounded less than enthusiastic. Andrew picked up on it.

"Hey, what's up? You usually groove on this kind of hype."

I changed my tone and put my thoughts in my back pocket, where they belonged.

"Everything's fine. We'll rock the house tonight!"

"Good. The doctor is in!" He had started calling me this after I passed my comprehensive exams.

Two men put their name on the waiting list for a table and sat at the bar. I introduced myself, but they didn't reciprocate. The one with the beard asked for a menu. They had a twenty-minute wait for a table and were interested in an appetizer.

"How are the hard-shells prepared? We are from the Chesapeake Bay area and are particular about our crabs," the Beard said.

"We steam them in Old Bay seasoning and beer."

He nodded knowingly and ordered a half dozen, a Baltimore brew for himself, and a glass of wine for his companion, following my suggestion. They watched Bruno put down the setup. They questioned him about every item, which was strange, since they supposedly knew all about eating hard-shells.

I became suspicious.

"What name did they give?" I asked the hostess.

"Smith."

I suggested that she have Bruno alert Andrew that the rumored reviewers might be in the house.

Meanwhile, at the university, Professors Higgins, Menlo, and Adams had convened their annual review of doctoral candidates. I could just picture it.

Higgins tapped his pen, shook his head, and stared at the ceiling while he began his rant. "What are we going to do about Rothberg?" He leaned back to the tipping point of his chair. "How is she ever going to do a dissertation pouring shots?"

"I had her lead a student-driven consulting project," Menlo said. "She did quite well." Menlo liked to argue with Higgins just for the sake of arguing.

"That's not the point. How does it look to have one of our candidates pushing booze?"

"Why, you never drink?" Menlo was beginning to enjoy himself.

Higgins said, "There are dues to pay, and she's not paying them."

"One ought not judge that what she does has no value until one sees what it is that she actually does," Adams, the youngest of the crew, said in a challenging tone.

"You can't think that this is a good thing. It's ridiculous," Higgins said, his hand rattling the change in his pocket.

"Let's find out." Menlo stood up, and the other two followed him through the door.

A few minutes later in they walked and sat next to the Beard and his companion at the bar.

"Oh, shit!" I muttered. For a moment I felt short of breath.

"What's up?" the hostess asked as she was picking up a drink order for the dining room.

"The miserable review committee. Adams, the youngest one—he's the only one in the entire faculty who believes that doctoral candidates are also people. The guy with the white hair, Menlo, he's the senior guy. The one with the comb-over, Higgins—he told me to quit this job today. Here they are, at my bar, the firing squad."

"What are you going to do?"

"Be who I am, a moving target. What else is there?"

She picked up the drink tray.

I walked over to the troika. "Good evening, gentlemen. What a surprise. It's nice to see you in my neck of the woods."

"Hello, Rothberg. We thought we'd stop in and discover the appeal of this place," Adams said with a smile. Higgins had a sarcastic gleam in his eye. Menlo was deadpan.

"Are you going to have something to eat at the bar with your drinks, or should I put you on the waiting list for a table?"

"No, we're going to sit here awhile," Adams said.

Higgins took out a small pad and his pen. My stomach dropped. Andrew and I would both be reviewed tonight.

"What do you recommend?" Menlo was leaning forward on his bar stool.

"How authentic do you want to be?" I was doing my best to hide the rattle in my brain.

"Why don't you decide how we would best experience the vision of this place," Adams suggested.

"Okay. One last question: Beer or wine?"

If they wanted to experience the Maryland Crab House, I was going to give it to them full-on. I asked Bruno to start them with crab cakes and Aunt Ray's she-crab soup, and white wine. Then I'd move them on to hard-shells and red wine.

As they ate their first course, I had a moment to really look at them. These three wise men, who had so much power over all the doctoral candidates in the program—who had so much power over such an important part of my life—were sitting in the only place I ever really felt safe and in control. They were there to judge me, to see whether I had learned anything of value. Whether I could really think or if I was just clever and gaming the system. Higgins had accused me of this when I'd passed my comprehensive exams. He thought that my doing well might have been the halo effect, where my personal charm influenced others' assessments of me. He said that my charisma and ability to think on my feet would have to translate into research and writing if I ever hoped to make an "incremental contribution to our models."

I was working my own model—ADVICE—and applying what I was learning every time I stepped behind that bar. For me, ideas were more useful when I could see them at work than when I merely hypothesized about how they might work in an academic setting.

I was taking Action by showing what I was capable of, such as how I got this job, how I got into the program, and how I passed my comprehensive exams.

Determination helped me achieve outcomes with civility, like getting Gina to leave Cincinnati and getting a dissertation topic accepted.

I had a Vision for my future, to become a professor, and was doing what I needed to get there by successfully engaging with this PhD program, just as Andrew had had a vision for surfside fare in Gramercy Park.

I tried to have Integrity, to own what was mine, to be honest and admit when I was wrong, and to do what it took to make things right.

I Communicated with much more than words, paying attention to all cues so that I could understand a situation for what it was, as I had learned the hard way from the bar fight.

And I demonstrated Empathy: I cared about the people I worked with, had helped Bruno move into a bartender role, had helped Andrew nurture and grow this business, and one day would help students reach the highest expression of what they could do and who they could become.

Yet in that moment of following my ADVICE, I realized that I couldn't do anything to impress them. And that I didn't want to. I realized that *I am who I am*, and that was going to have to be good enough. The cloud lifted, and I stopped caring that they were there. I had pushed my way into the program, but if the shoe really didn't fit, I wasn't going to force my foot in any further. I could always find another set of shoes. Tonight I was going to stand comfortably in my own.

ADVICE: Be who you are.

It was a busier-than-usual Tuesday night for us. Andrew was sweating it out in the kitchen. He needed a good review to help him open another restaurant. I was sweating it out at the bar, hoping that "the Committee" would let me move forward into a dissertation. I had the bar running like a charm. The dinners Andrew plated were beautiful. The reviewers saw it all. Would it be enough?

The Committee left after three courses, coffee, and key lime pie. Menlo paid the bill, and Higgins, having scribbled on his pad all evening, put it back in his pocket.

"See you tomorrow in my office, Rothberg" was how Higgins said good night. Adams waved, Menlo nodded, and they were gone.

A half hour later the bar was almost empty, and I was polishing the top-shelf bottles. Adams came back and stood at the service end.

"I didn't expect to see you here again," I said as I kept wiping off the cognacs.

"What exactly is the vision for this place?" he said. He was cordial, inquisitive, and gentle.

"Chesapeake Bay surfside in Gramercy Park." This was the easiest question I would ever be asked by a member of the Committee.

"That fits. Do you have a minute to talk?" he said. He remained standing.

"Yeah, sure. Do I need to sit down for this?" I was half joking, but my mind was racing.

"We saw what you know, what you do. We're aware of how hard it is to create an environment where people feel welcome. Good job."

"Thanks. So what does Higgins want with me tomorrow?"

"Don't worry about it. He's just being Higgins." Adams smiled.

"The notebook—he was writing the whole time."

"A shopping list, 'The Star-Spangled Banner,' the alphabet— nothing of consequence. We talked on the way back to Penn Station. We realize that you do learn differently than the typical candidate. You haven't worked with us in our research running surveys or writing articles. You don't spend your summers in the library. And you have picked the strangest topics to write your papers on. I still wonder how you pulled off 'Zen and Creative Problem Solving in Management.' But when we put you in a situation where you can apply what we teach, in simulations, or on consulting projects—or here in this place—we see that you do indeed learn."

Andrew came out from the kitchen. He was sweaty and messy and really happy.

"We rocked it tonight, didn't we?"

"Your food was beautiful, Andrew. Congratulations."

"And you had things running like clockwork. Again. THE DOCTOR WAS IN THE HOUSE!" He gave me a hard high five.

"Not yet, but she will be soon." Adams said, nodding at me, and left the bar.

"Who was that?"

"The fair one. A long story."

Leadership Is More Than Management

To lead others, you have to know where you stand yourself. A leader's worldview attracts those who are a good fit and provides them with a clear pathway for fulfilling expectations. And there are many pathways. Higgins's conviction was that doctoral candidates needed to conduct research with faculty. Menlo valued practical experience. Adams believed that people have unique styles. They were all correct. To be awarded a PhD, I needed to blend these expectations in a way that was true to myself, just as Andrew had to for a successful restaurant. He had believed in the Chesapeake Bay concept and, although a skilled classical chef, he needed to demonstrate his vision to the reviewers with authentic food. I needed to blend throwing elbows, pouring drinks, and managing the flow of the dining room with theory and structure.

At the core, leaders are teachers. They don't try to force a square peg into a round hole. They find a way to fit what is needed with the best a person brings to the table. I was always a kinetic learner: I needed to experience something, to see how it works, to really *get* it. I could read a management book and intellectually understand the concepts, but when I put them to work behind the bar, or as a junior consultant, that's when they clicked into place. The basketball courts, the restaurants, the bar—these were my laboratories.

Leaders understand that people learn differently and use what they learn differently. They don't try to create images of themselves in others. Instead, they see people as individuals—who a person is and what he or she can do—and they bring out the best in others.

As an explorer and a doer, I couldn't become someone I was not just to achieve a goal. I had to find a way to stand in my own shoes and do what was required of me with integrity and excellence. The more I understood that there could be a happy medium between who the Committee wanted me to be and who I was becoming, the easier it became to dedicate myself to finishing the degree. I realized that if I wanted to move ahead, I had to better blend who I was and who they were.

I used the "two and out" rule: if I say something and there's no agreement, then maybe I didn't phrase it clearly, so I try again. If there's still no agreement the second time, then it's because whomever I'm talking to or doing something with doesn't concur with my view. That's when I stop trying. If I were to continue, I would be perceived as a nag and be tuned out anyway. So "two and out."

My first two proposals were on strategic issues, and Higgins rejected them. For my third dissertation proposal, I read everything Higgins had ever written, then found a way to put my twist on his work and make "an incremental contribution" to his models. I looked at his theories about success and failure and proposed to study personal well-being, how achieving success in something that is not in alignment with one's value system can affect satisfaction and happiness. He accepted this as a subject. He still made me jump through hoops—I had to rewrite the foundational chapters three times even after they had been approved—but I was on my way. I stood in my own shoes and tied them with their laces. Great leaders utilize the diversity of a person's contributions, not only those they are most familiar with. And sometimes the most meaningful contribution can come from differences or even conflict. When people agree about a goal but disagree about how to best achieve it, more information can be learned than might have been the case if there had been total agreement. Here conflict is productive and can yield a better decision.

Conflict is disruptive when disagreement revolves around a goal. The key is to find pathways of agreement, regardless of how small, and then move ahead and build from there. Sometimes you have to compromise and abandon preferences, but if the goal is clear and a road can be built that aligns with your sense of direction and value, you can get to where you are going.

After the Bar

Becoming from the Inside Out

Within a year of my joining the faculty at Marist College, the academic vice president nominated me for a position on the board of directors for the Taconic Independent Practice Association (Taconic IPA). The Taconic IPA is a not-for-profit organization representing five thousand doctors across the greater Hudson Valley whose mission is to provide quality patient care.

Taconic IPA had hired the consulting firm KPMG to help them create a more productive board. Working with them for almost a year,

KPMG recommended that they hire an executive team and restructure their board, cutting it from twenty-two physicians to eight and adding one nonphysician. The consultant suggested they reach out to Marist College to find this layperson and I was nominated and chosen to serve.

When I joined the new board of nine, they had just hired their first executive director, who brought along with him a new medical director. The physicians were used to being masters of the universe, decision makers in their offices and operating rooms, experts in their field. When it came to running an organization and an executive team, however, they were naïve. They also didn't realize what it would be like to have an outspoken businessperson in their midst. I was demanding about the kind of hard information we needed in our monthly meetings, direct in what the implications of the data were, and challenging in my questions. My purpose was to help them learn a new way to look at performance.

By the fourth board meeting, I had questions about the executive director. I hadn't been part of the interview process to hire him, and didn't know much about his background. He seemed to be the wrong person in the wrong position at the wrong time. He didn't understand how to present financial statements coherently. He had little to contribute in board committee meetings. At our marketing and physician-education committee meetings, all he did was take notes. When he offered to come to my home and help me rake leaves, I knew that I had to take action.

I suggested that the board run a thorough six-month performance review. I interviewed people from every touch point of the executive director's job: subordinates, physicians, insurance company executives. Everyone thought he was in over his head. I suggested that we put him on six months' probation. The board members were shocked by my report, except for one: the vice chairman, Dr. A. John Blair III.

From the start, John had the same questions I did. A general surgeon, John was the business-practice manager for his medical group and had a penchant for quality improvement. As a medical resident he had published on the topic; as a surgeon he joined the hospital's quality-assurance team. He joined Taconic IPA to help set protocols and create guidelines to improve community health.

Instead of being taken aback by my abrupt and succinct report, John realized that I was pushing for better quality in our executive leader. He and I would confer before and after the board meetings. I had the sense that he was engaging in a form of Vulcan mind meld, gleaning everything he could from my strategic brain. By the time John became chairman of the board, we had dismissed the Taconic IPA executive director, and John wanted to take on this role. We needed to convince the other board members that his practice-management talents could successfully transfer to running Taconic IPA. After he had articulated his vision, his goals for the year, and a plan to execute them, John became Taconic IPA's leader.

An excellent surgeon, John also quickly demonstrated that he was an excellent executive. He was strategic, and had a long-term view of what the health care environment was becoming. John understood that both quality outcomes and cost containment were needed to serve the ever-increasing demand from an aging population. He was a risk-taker and an innovator, pursuing new roles that stretched his skill set. A masterful negotiator with the key insurer, MVP, he achieved a better contractual relationship for the doctors and implemented quality initiatives.

Beyond his management and negotiation acumen, John was a visionary. He saw the potential for medical technology to improve the delivery of quality health care for both patients and insurance companies before it was on most medical practitioners' radar. We spoke often about new business models. It was sometimes hard for me to remember that he was a surgeon and not an entrepreneur.

In the 1970s and 1980s, hospitals used information systems to control costs, primarily in admissions and billing. Health care mavericks began expanding this role to patient care in the 1990s. John was a very early proponent of creating electronic versions of patients' medical histories that would follow them to their health care providers, whether they were physicians, hospitals, or nursing homes. He predicted that electronic health records would facilitate improvement of community health care while managing costs. He understood the challenges of bringing health-information technologies to store, share, and analyze health information into doctors' offices, and the need for it to work seamlessly between hospitals, laboratories, and pharmacies.

Two things needed to happen simultaneously for electronic health records and health-information technologies to be adopted early and earnestly in the Hudson Valley: a partnership with MVP insurance, which collected patient data, and a deliberate plan of action for John to become a face for the way technology can transform community medicine. We made a plan to do both.

In 2001, MVP and Taconic IPA formed a partnership, MedAllies, to promote and facilitate electronic health record adoption among doctors. John fought for the position of president. Who better to understand the challenges of a medical practice and patient needs than John, a physician, since he had proven himself deft at managing the challenges of Taconic IPA and had a clear vision of how he would get the medical community to work with MedAllies? The CEO of MVP was initially reluctant to give John this role, wanting instead to recruit a more experienced executive, but ultimately was persuaded and, in time, became one of John's greatest supporters. Years later, John would leave his practice to concentrate his energy at MedAllies full-time. And in 2009, when MVP disengaged from the partnership, John invested his own resources to keep MedAllies afloat.

Dr. John Blair also became a sought-after speaker at medical technology conferences, an expert witness before Congress, and a driving force in other not-for-profit organizations seeking to create community health care initiatives. For instance, in the Hudson Valley Initiative, which explores ways to improve health care delivery in the Hudson Valley, John helped forge a partnership with Weill Cornell Medical College to independently evaluate and validate research attesting to the success of health initiatives in both patient quality and financial outcomes. MedAllies has been selected as one of three networks to seamlessly connect electronic health records and health-information technologies across different medical-community stakeholders. MedAllies is one of the leading national Direct Network providers.

The surgeon became a practice manager, then a board chairman, then an executive director, then an expert speaker, entrepreneur, and company president. In all of these roles, he maintained his soul and passion for improving the quality of care for patients and communities. When John stopped practicing medicine, it was to step out of one set of shoes completely and into another.

It's common to stereotype a person, to look at their title or their "label" and then create a story of who you believe that person to be. Considering how much information any of us processes on a given day, how many different things we pay attention to at any given moment, it is not surprising that our minds would create ways to manage information efficiently. We talk about people as "givers" or "takers," "thinkers" or "doers," the "good witch" or the "bad witch." We use generational labels such as "baby boomers," "millennials," and "the silent generation" to assign traits, preferences, and behaviors. We think we know someone by their occupational title, religion, or national origin. Yet these mental maps can be inaccurate, limiting our understanding of people. Logos, taglines, and positioning statements can communicate myriad details, but they can also limit our perspective.

Maybe, instead of a stereotype, or a scripted brand attribute, or a professional title, we can make the effort to understand our core qualities, salient beliefs, and heartfelt values, which are not beholden to a category, a type, or an expected behavior. The girl from the Lower East Side can work uptown and pursue a PhD in a predominantly male field. A physician can be a thought leader, businessperson, and trailblazer. Standing in your own shoes is not so much a matter of knowing whether you are a sneaker or a boot person, someone who prefers heels or flats, as it is understanding your foot and what that foot might choose to fashion in different situations at different times.

At some point on the path to achieving the dream, you will make compromises. The key to good leadership is understanding which ones to make. In each ingredient of the leadership ADVICE cocktail, there are choices. How to best communicate? How to make difficult choices? What type of action to take? The key is to find a way to blend what matters most to you personally with what is essential for work. When we do so with the right balance of expectations for our companies and ourselves, we are able to grow and succeed in a manner that allows us to become the best performers that we can be.

It's easy to get lost in organizations, to get lost in the demands that a "grown-up" life comes with. We are products of all the leaders, pathfinders, and pillars, formal and informal, who have been part of our lives. The visionary at work, the teacher who expands possibilities, the courageous public figure, the caring parent, the friend who lifts us to a new level—we push to live up to their expectations, hopes, and ambitions for us. But this has to be in balance with the hopes and goals we have for ourselves.

Leaders know who they are, what they stand for, what they are willing and not willing to do. And while this may change over time, it does so as a product of experience, from an understanding of and regard for the complex person who is evolving, outside the brand, the logo, the stereotype. Leaders have the courage to be genuine. They have the wisdom to encourage authenticity in others. And sometimes, like Professor Adams or Dr. A. John Blair, to open the door to make it all work.

The Drink

BRAIN SQUEEZE

3 ounces spiced rum

1 teaspoon orange bitters

3 cardamom pods, crushed

1 cinnamon stick

Blend the rum and bitters slowly. Add ice, then the cardamom and cinnamon stick. (You may want to sprinkle a little cumin on top.) Infuse with authentic self. Serve with a conviction sidecar.

Having the conviction to be who you are and the courage to accept difference in others is hard work. In the inner chatter, it is not always easy to ferret out what is yours and what belongs to others. You have to squeeze your brain and ask: *What really matters?*

- Spiced rum: it is used as a medium of exchange. Etymologists trace the name "rum" to mean "the best" or "strong." It's for recognizing what to take and what to leave behind.
- Orange bitters: made from peels of Seville oranges and spices, it is dry and brings out the flavor in other ingredients (and people).
- Cumin: around since before the second millennium BC, it is thought to improve the immune system. It is aromatic and flavorful, and its very presence can change the path of whatever it is mixed with; do so with ease.
- Cardamom seeds in a pod: they are pungent, aromatic, and thought to relieve congestion and to create clarity in making choices.
- Infusion of authentic self: being who you are instead of who you or others think you should be. Sit and seep into the mixture.
- Conviction sidecar: holding a strong belief. Should accompany what really matters and be readily accessible for rimming the glass or adding a stronger squeeze.

Here's to standing firmly in your own shoes!

ADVICE: Shape-Shifting

MY FIFTH YEAR TENDING bar at the Maryland Crab House found me with an approved topic and deep into writing my dissertation. My final hoop for the PhD, dissertating (an actual word), had me spinning in uncertainty. Behind the bar, I was in control. I knew who I was. While I couldn't predict what would happen during any given shift, I had developed the confidence that I would figure it out. There were lessons everywhere in what worked and what didn't. Sometimes it was fun, sometimes it was hard, but I always felt as if I was learning how to get things done by myself and with others.

In dissertating, I was on less-solid ground. I wasn't in control of all the moving parts. The Committee was. There were five people on my thesis committee. Three—Professors Higgins, Menlo, and Adams—had prodded me along from the start. They were now joined by Professor Lee, a statistics expert, and Professor Nador, an outside reviewer from a different university. Each wanted something different on any given day. Professor Nador thought my literature review and hypotheses were very good and recommended me to the doctoral consortium of the Academy of Management. Professor Higgins thought the paper needed to be totally rewritten. Professor Menlo wanted me to run analysis-of-variance statistics. Professor Lee thought it should be a moderated multiple-regression analysis. Professor Adams wanted a graphic display and table of my research model. Professor Lee thought it should be in narrative form. These might seem like contradictory demands, and they were. Each couldn't have been more different in what he wanted me to do. Yet each had to agree on and then approve the placement of every comma. Luckily for me, the restaurant kept me grounded.

Early on a Friday evening, the Five Guys came in for their ritual of steamed dozens. They asked about "the monster," their nickname for my dissertation. I told them about my latest hurdle: Lee, the statistics guy, had gone on a six-week vacation to Europe without approving my model for managing the data that I needed to analyze.

"You ever gonna finish?"

I told them that it depended on the day. On some days I felt confident in what I was writing and that I would indeed make a contribution to the field. On other days—usually after a meeting with Higgins, during which he would make me rewrite a chapter for the fourth time or tell me that I needed to dive into yet another school of thought—I felt as if it would never end.

"If I ever get to be a full-fledged faculty member, I am never going to make students squirm like a mouse with its tail caught in the door," I said, wiping the counter around them.

"Have you ever taught?" asked Minnesota Five Guy, rinsing Old Bay seasoning off his fingers in the water bowl.

"I loved being a day-camp counselor. Does that count?" I handed him some napkins.

"Are you going to have your students make jewelry boxes out of Popsicle sticks?" he asked as he picked up his mallet again.

"Truth is, I actually started teaching three weeks ago. I'm an adjunct instructor at Polytechnic Institute of NYU, out on Long Island, teaching organizational behavior to engineers old enough to be my dad who work at Grumman and Fairchild. But, honestly, it's not that different from making jewelry boxes from Popsicle sticks," I replied.

When I had started talking theoretically about leadership, motivation, and perception, the engineers looked at me like I had two heads. I decided to talk to them in their language. I turned all of the theories that I was teaching into systems diagrams.

"Then I found these experiential activities with Tinkertoys and Lincoln Logs. I had them design, build, and deconstruct in different ways to demonstrate what I was trying to explain."

"Where did you learn to do that?" Minnesota Five Guy asked.

"Here, behind the bar."

We started to reminisce about some of the things we'd been through. I had met the Five Guys my first night working for free at the restaurant when it was still Cincinnati. Their friend from the Jersey Shore had inadvertently helped orchestrate Gina's departure. They were there during the Maryland Crab House's surprise launch. They had sat at the bar when the blue moon was full and strange people meandered in and sometimes rattled the staff. We had all learned from the bar fight that communication is so much more than words. As we talked about all the lessons we'd learned, I realized that learning is cumulative. Each event informs the next one. Each experience is an opportunity to learn, and learning is never done; it's a process, not a product.

"How'd you land this teaching gig?" they asked.

Russ Walker, a professor I had met four years earlier while working as a doctoral assistant in the management department at Baruch College, always asked me how things were going when he picked up his mail. One day he came into school wearing an old tweed jacket and striped tie, the knot too fat for the fashion, carrying a big plastic garbage bag stuffed with academic publications slung over his shoulder like Santa Claus.

"Fifty-two papers, to be exact. This was the only way I could think to carry them all in here," said this smart man. He was both halves of the Odd Couple: he had the neuroses of Felix and the presentation of Oscar. "I am being reviewed for promotion."

Three weeks later, and two years before the doctoral review committee came in for their surprise visit, Professor Russ Walker sat at the end of the bar at the Maryland Crab House.

"Professor Walker! I didn't know that you knew about this place," I exclaimed.

"My dear, the whole faculty knows that you work here. Be careful, those barracudas are not happy about it. And *please* call me Russ."

He ordered a glass of red wine and sat at the bar sulking. The senior faculty had denied his promotion. He felt that they treated him like an outsider because he was a sociologist. Because he didn't wear Brooks Brothers suits. Because he wore Timberland walking shoes.

"You need to be playing a better political game than I did," Russ said, pointing his finger at me.

"What do you mean?" I asked, a little nervous now that a lot of people at the college knew I was tending bar. The senior faculty expected doctoral students to work for them, running statistics and writing literature reviews for articles we would never be credited for.

"You need experience."

"This bar is an experience, believe me."

"I schlepped trays of food in the Catskill Mountains as a kid, too. But you need to experience the field that you want to enter, to see if you would really like it. You need to start teaching."

"That makes sense. How do I do that?" I wasn't ready yet, but it was never too early to start the paperwork. I wondered why in the past two years none of the faculty in my graduate program offered to help me do this.

Although he was thirty years my senior, Russ and I became friends. He helped me perfect a résumé and cover letter. When I finished my course work two years later, I sent them to ten schools across the tristate area where he had friends. Polytechnic on Long Island invited me for an interview. A pudgy man with glasses told me that I was too inexperienced for the position, but they must have been desperate, because they called me five days before the fall semester began and offered me the job.

I refreshed the Five Guys' drinks and told them the rest of Russ Walker's story.

In the two years between the time he helped me with my résumé and my landing my first teaching job, Russ hadn't gotten over his colleagues' rejection of him. I tried to persuade him to broaden his horizons beyond his Introduction to Management classroom. I'd circle activities in *New York* magazine and new job postings in the *Chronicle of Higher Education*, and I introduced him to people at the bar. He didn't budge until I brought him a flyer about an inexpensive trip for academics to France during spring break. I had considered going myself for the stop in Paris, but I couldn't swing it. Russ decided to go because of the stop in Normandy.

Amelie Paul, a girl my age who lived in Paris, was the tour guide, and she and Russ had a romance. He was in love and returned from his trip pining for her. It took me the rest of the semester to persuade him to return to Paris. I shot down every excuse that kept him in the same sorry spot: he was tenured, yeah, but they would never promote him; his children were here, but they were grown and living their own lives; and so on. After two months of my nagging him, he accepted a visiting position as the dean of student affairs at an American university in Paris. A couple of years after that, they both moved to the United States, where

Amelie Paul enrolled in a graduate program in museum studies and Russ became the dean of a management department at a private college in Queens. They married soon after.

ADVICE: Get out of your own way.
Change can change everything.

Toward the end of my fifth year at the Maryland Crab House, and my sixth year in the PhD program, I could see the light at the end of the tunnel, and it wasn't an oncoming train. I was gaining traction on my dissertation. With luck, I would be done with "the monster" within two years. On a cool spring night, Russ and Amelie Paul came to the Maryland Crab House. Russ had news.

"I'm changing programs again. I'll be teaching at a college in New Jersey in the fall."

I poured them each a glass of red wine and said, "That was fast."

"Private college isn't for me. I'm going to a small public institution that's going to try for business accreditation." He was excited.

"Russ, tell her why we are here!" Amelie Paul said as she nudged him.

"They're looking for a full-time assistant professor to teach management, organization behavior, and strategy courses. I told them about you."

It was suddenly hard to breathe. My stomach felt queasy. I wanted to run out the front door. I turned away and started shuffling through a drawer, rearranged some bottles, and then faced them again.

"I haven't finished dissertating. How can I manage that and a full-time position?" I tried to sound matter-of-fact.

"You'd have to give up bartending." Clearly, Russ had thought this through. "You have to make the leap sometime. This is a quiet school. The teaching load is heavy, but the people are nice, no barracudas"—code for people like the Committee. "It's a perfect place to start your career and finish up your PhD," he said gently. He recognized that I was unnerved.

"I really appreciate you thinking about me. I'm not sure this is the right time—"

"Helen, this is the right time. These types of opportunities do not come along very often. You don't have to move to Kansas to get your first job. It is not a pressure cooker. And I'll be there to help you navigate. Update your résumé and I'll send it with a cover letter."

I agreed to get my paperwork in order and then we dropped the subject. But it stayed with me for the rest of the night.

Andrew called; he was running late for a meeting we had set up to talk about scheduling a private party. He was just leaving his new restaurant and asked if I'd wait for him. I was relieved to have the time. My Armagnac and I had a lot to sort out. As I sat on a stool, staring at the shining bottles behind the dimly lit bar, I realized that this place was home.

It was here, behind this oak bar, that I had discovered so many things about myself and life and making things work. At the Maryland Crab House, I knew exactly what I could do and what I could get others to do. Was it possible to do that all over again?

"Thanks for waiting," Andrew said. I hadn't heard him let himself in through the locked door.

"Where are you?" he asked, and nudged me to get me out of my thoughts.

"I'm here," I said and took a deep breath. "How's Steak Frites?"

"A slow night, but it picked up." He looked at the register receipts from the evening's business that I had waiting on the bar next to his cognac. "Looks like we had a good night. Why the long face?"

"I'm thinking about what's next."

"Ah. I've been waiting for this," he said. I looked at him but didn't say anything. "I didn't think that the doctor was going to run my bar forever. Even if I wished for it."

"I'm good at it."

"Yes, you are. And you'll be good at what's next, too."

I swirled the amber liquid around the snifter and watched how it made legs as it slowly settled back to the bottom of the glass.

"My friend Russ told me about a full-time assistant professorship across the river."

"When does it start?"

"Assuming I get it, five months from now, in September."

"When have you not gotten something you put your mind to? You'll walk out of the interview with an offer, and not have to work for free to get it." Andrew smiled at me, and we sat and sipped from our snifters. The silence between us was both comfortable and uncomfortable; we were two friends readying for separate travels. Andrew put down his drink and stood to look at me.

"Most people who work here have a dream. You are going to live yours. I am really happy that I got to play a part in your journey."

"You may never know how big a part it is," I said, my throat getting tight. I took a deep breath. "Thank you, Andrew. You have been one of my great teachers."

"And you, one of mine."

We clinked glasses, shut the lights, and pulled the gate down on the Maryland Crab House.

In September, as I drove to New Jersey for the first day of class, I thought about being the kind of professor I had rarely experienced myself: approachable, practical, supportive, and encouraging. Making people yawn and watch the clock would be a crime. I wanted to take all my history, all my experience—all that I was—put it in my new suit and pumps, and make the lessons come alive. I wanted to bring out the best in my students. I wanted them to bring out the best in me.

My first classroom had thirty students seated at very small desks. I could see their surprise when I walked in. I was young, English was my first language, and I wasn't wearing flats. I put my briefcase on a chair, wrote my name on the blackboard, and moved the lectern out of the way. I sat on top of the desk, looked around the room, took a deep breath, smiled, and began my first lecture:

"Everything I know about leadership, about being successful, I learned as a bartender."

Leadership Is Not Management

Shape-shifting—moving from one role to another—requires getting out of your own way. It is a dynamic interplay between who you are and who you will become; what stays the same and what transforms. There's uncertainty in whether what worked in one environment will work in another. Whether your friends will still be your friends as you grow and learn. Whether the way you look at the world will still be relevant. Whether you will be good enough. And that's why change takes courage.

My relationship with the bar extended beyond my technical competency, beyond my ability to manage the waitstaff and satisfy my customers. I was needed. I had built a community. We relied on one another, shared our lives with one another, and cared about one another. I later realized that part of my fearful reaction about moving on was leaving the attention that I knew awaited me every time I walked through the door. My customers saw who I was, appreciated who I was, and enjoyed sharing time with me. I was the center of their attention as they were mine. What would life be like without this?

I had invested almost six years trying to earn the credentials I needed to become a professor. What if the students didn't like my style? What if the faculty thought my range of experience was inadequate for what I was teaching? What if what I learned from junior consulting projects and internships and bartending didn't transfer into my toolbox? What if I was a really good bartender and not a good professor? And, most frightening of all, what if I didn't like teaching? Then what? What does it mean to invest so much in something that has a disappointing return?

The beauty of it was that I now knew I could always pick a new destination and find my way there. That even if the outcome was disappointing, I still learned, grew, and endured, and I could do it again.

There's another side to *What if. . . ?*—one that most people don't readily consider: *What if. . . ?* can actually be positive. What if all I had learned translated into an overflowing toolbox? What if I could step into my shape-shifting pumps and be an engaging and insightful teacher and a mindful colleague? What if I approached shape-shifting with optimism, with the confidence that I had worked hard, had prepared, and was ready. And this was where I had landed.

———

To lead yourself through change with confidence and optimism, you need ADVICE: Action, Determination, Vision, Integrity, Communication, and Empathy. There is no room for complacency, negativity, or comfort. Courage is driven by the hope of something better, not the fear of being inadequate. Each opportunity offers a chance to develop a part of yourself, to apply all that you think you are and all that you will learn that you are. New pathways open to discovering parts of yourself that you may not have even known were there. Over time, with each new shape, another type of confidence is achieved: the confidence that, whatever happens, the grit, brawn, knowledge, soothsaying, deeper view, humor, inquisitiveness, humility, honesty, drive, concentration, or soul-searching—whatever is needed—will find its way into the toolbox.

Andrew was a born shape-shifter. In each new restaurant, he incorporated the lessons he had learned from the ones before, changing yet staying the same. He opened City Crab and Seafood, true to his Chesapeake Bay theme, but with three hundred seats. And there were more restaurants after that. Andrew, in building what currently is known as the Flatiron Restaurant Group, lived each ingredient in the ADVICE model. And I got to live many of them with him.

We choose to stay the same or to learn and grow. While Confucius reminds us that "wherever you go there you are," there are also parts of ourselves that shift with new experiences. And choosing new experiences alters our shapes, so that we are the same but different.

After the Bar

Becoming Is a Process, Not a Product, Even for Organizations

For decades, David Bell was a thought leader and CEO in the advertising sector. He was, and still is, playful, brilliant, and insightful, and a creative executive, mentor, and friend. I had the good fortune to work with him as a consultant. For my first assignment, we hosted an off-site meeting where we brought together a band of thoroughbred executives to ignite innovative competitive thinking. As an icebreaker at the opening dinner, we assigned each person a fellow thoroughbred to introduce. The only rule was that they couldn't use the person's résumé. We thought this would be fun as well as give us a quick sense of the players.

I asked for the list of attendees, their agency positions, and their tenures at the company. I wanted to put together people who didn't know each other well. Dana Maiman, a vice president for a health care advertising arm of a major agency, was on the list. I had first met Dana my freshman year at Stuyvesant High School in Manhattan, a specialized high school concentrating on mathematics and the sciences. It was all-male until 1969, when they lost *Alice DeRivera v. New York City Board of Education* and admitted fourteen girls. When I entered in 1973, girls represented about one-quarter of the student body. From all five boroughs, we pioneer girls bonded in the park behind the school, at the local coffee shop, over grilled-cheese sandwiches in the Fugue Bar & Grill, and in the bathrooms with urinals (we thought they were ashtrays). We confounded some of the male gym teachers with our three-week-long menstruations and moodiness. Some of the teachers longed for the old days when they were simply preparing young men to be the "future leaders of the world." Boys were not as complicated, the older teachers said.

Luckily for those girls who were athletes, Mr. McGrath, a stocky, dark-haired man who was as quick to shout as to smile, was supportive. While the girls were relegated to the small gym, he let us use the track in the "real" gym. Dana Maiman and I loved to run and jump; hurdles and long jump were my focus, and we became close competitors in the 440 relay.

We wanted a jacket and a letter, just like the ones the boys' teams had.

A girl could get a jacket by managing a boys' team and earn a letter if the team did, but that wasn't good enough for Dana and me. In a school filled with brainiacs, if you weren't on the chess team, or winning the Math Olympiad in Yugoslavia, or blowing something up in the lab while chasing a Westinghouse scholarship, you were an athlete and had a jacket. Whenever we won, we earned points, and with enough points we could earn a letter and wear it on our jackets. That meant something.

So we pestered Mr. McGrath, who wasn't ready to take on a bunch of girls as a team. We did more and said less. We were determined. We had a vision. We began working out with the boys' track and field team—the whole workout. The captain, Steve, thought this was cool and taught Dana and me the right way to pace hurdles. When Dede Nethersole decided to join us and sprinted past a couple of the boys, Mr. McGrath took notice.

During our sophomore season, more girls showed up on the track. Dana and I presented Mr. McGrath with all the completed paperwork to create a new team, and we persuaded one of the female gym instructors to co-captain. Every day we pushed Mr. McGrath to sign. After two weeks he did, and the Stuyvesant High School Girl's Track & Field team was born. Dana and I designed a beautiful blue satin jacket with a white satin stripe and red trim running down the sleeve, with a big winged foot on the back framed with "Stuyvesant Track." Our letter *S* was red with blue trim. Now we had to win or place in enough meets to earn the letter.

During our inaugural season, I tore my hamstring in gym and couldn't compete. I came back in my junior year but had lost speed. In my senior year I was jumping but was not on the competitive relay team. With two meets to go for the season, I was short six points for my letter. I was also managing the boys' swim team, so I could have earned a letter that way, but for me, that didn't have integrity.

Then Dede was out sick for the penultimate meet. Dana, the team captain, urged Mr. McGrath to put me in the 440 hurdles relay in

Dede's place. With Dede out, we knew we couldn't win, but we could place. Mr. McGrath let me run third.

Our first runner took the lead. The second runner finished in third place. I finished my leg of the race in fourth place. Dana was the closer, and after I passed the baton to her, she ran the best time of her high school career. The team came in second. In the final meet of the season, I came in second in the running long jump and earned my *S*.

Now, for the agency's opening dinner—remembering how Dana had fought for me to run that race and earn my letter—I assigned her David Bell to introduce. Her description of him was humorous, thoughtful, and brilliant. Later, David asked me why I paired the two of them and I told him about the letter. Dana is now CEO of the agency's advertising arm. She earned another *S*.

———

Organizations shape-shift. New leaders bring with them new structures, strategies, and sensibilities. Cultures shape-shift, too. A court order had forced Stuyvesant High School to admit girls. The structure had to adapt, providing bathrooms and locker rooms, but the culture was much slower to do so. Advocating for girls' sports meant pushing for cultural change. It meant pressing for recognition that girls had some of the same attributes that the boys had: we were smart, competitive, and resourceful, "future leaders of the world."

Organizations can shape-shift passively through adaptation over time, with small changes cumulatively creating a new form. Or they can shape-shift and transform purposefully. When they do, leaders have to have courage and act quickly for their organizations to survive and thrive. David Bell signaled a shift in culture when he participated in the icebreaker, communicating his willingness to work with his rising stars and be open to their contributions. While it was a subtle move, other leaders hadn't taken it before. It ushered in a different culture in which junior executives more openly expressed their opinions and took risks without the fear of retribution.

Organizations face the same challenges individuals do, such as uncertainty about what will stay the same and what will change. So leading an organization—and a culture—through shape-shifting, through major change, also takes ADVICE: Action, Determination, Vision, Integrity, Communication, and Empathy. Leaders answer "No" with "Why not?"; "Not now" with "When?"; "It can't be done" with "Let's see." They recognize the many wildflowers in the field— those who may have different viewpoints, unique ways of doing things, dreams—and ensure that they have ample sunshine, water, and wind to grow and spread their magic. This is how they cultivate new ideas and new ways of doing things to provide opportunities for people to dare to become more. This is how they create great organizations.

The Drink

GRAND STREET PLUS

3 ounces vodka

½ ounce St-Germain

½ ounce Alizé Red Passion

3 tablespoons water

2 tablespoons Italian lemon ice

4 ripe blueberries

Blend the ingredients. Add a twist of ADVICE with a courage sidecar. Splash with joy. Serve chilled.

We are who we were and also who we will become. Great leaders lead from their roots and with the new tools that come with success and failure. The shapes they take—familiar (Alizé to create pinkness) and different (St-Germain to add the bouquet of elderflowers)—are a result of moving through uncertainty with the will to emerge as evolved versions of themselves. They stand in their own shoes, perhaps with new laces and newly polished, ready for whatever comes next.

- Vodka: a solid yet flexible base that can take on many different mixers or stand alone.
- St-Germain: made from elderflowers, it is aromatic with many undertones; can stand alone or mix well with others.
- Alizé Red Passion: it promotes a healthy heart and healthy systems to keep things clear and enable blending.
- Splash of water: it creates smoothness without changing character.
- Italian lemon ice: good roots from the neighborhood, it is refreshing and bold.
- Ripe blueberries: a summer superfruit with anti-inflammatory (keeps things calm) and antioxidant (keeps things healthy) properties.
- Twist of ADVICE: beyond good management, the signature of leadership, essential for transformation.
- Courage sidecar: embracing what's next.
- Splash of joy: why not!

Here's to wherever you go, there you are—but better!

Afterword: Raising the Bar

WE LIVE BUSY LIVES—AT work, at home, at play. And sometimes, between getting the quarterly report done, engaging with clients, writing reviews, ordering supplies, arranging for shipments, grading papers, or doing whatever else work demands—along with getting a child to soccer, a parent to a doctor, a friend to a procedure, yourself to the gym or yoga, or maybe just walking the dog—there's a moment where you wonder, *How did I get here?* And when you think about what you can do differently, with student loans, a mortgage, a car payment, tuition, tutors, dental bills, and elder care, there doesn't seem to be time, energy, or resource wiggle room to do anything but what you *are* doing. You put one foot in front of the other, led by conflicting demands that even in a satisfying career or joyous personal life can feel overwhelming. As if there is not one more thing that can be pushed in. As if this is all there can be.

But there is more. There's ADVICE. You can lead yourself.

Somewhere in the overlapping systems of life, you can take action. You can choose to do something big, like change jobs if you are unhappy, or something small, like get up a half hour earlier each day to stretch, walk, or just hear the silence in your own head. Sometimes the thing to do is to purposefully do nothing. Not to avoid something, but when uncertain about which path to take, to wait and watch. Like a race car driver, "when in doubt, both feet out": if you don't know whether to brake or shift, take both feet off the pedals and see what the car does. Then you will know what action to take. And then take it.

Have DETERMINATION: Find a way to make things happen with ingenuity and civility. You don't need to use others as a stepping-stone to find higher ground. Be innovative in engaging the best of what you bring to the table and see it through.

Have VISION: Drive your actions and provide a purpose for your determination. Reach up, for a promotion or a raise, or reach out, expanding your sphere of experience and influence.

Have INTEGRITY: Ground the actions you take, the visions you create, the determination you engender, in order to move onward in integrity. Be honest, own what is yours, don't play into drama, see failure as an opportunity to learn, and remember what you stand for in your best version of yourself.

COMMUNICATE: Communication is complex. It's easy to create misunderstanding, with others and yourself. If you come from a place of integrity and want to understand and be understood, then you will have the patience to listen, the intention to be present, and the action of paying attention to all that surrounds a given situation.

Foster EMPATHY: Creating understanding will come not only from being attentive but also from caring: caring about whether you understand or are understood; caring about how your actions, your choices, affect others; caring about the people you engage with. Standing in their shoes, not just viewing from your own perch, does a lot to foster a sense of connection and community.

In leading yourself down the pathway to be the fullest expression of the person you want to be, you won't need to be led by others.

In August 2014, the *New York Times*, the *Economist*, Forbes.com, and many other business publications ran obituaries for Warren Bennis, the godfather of leadership theory and practice. Mr. Bennis had come to believe that leadership was driven by self-discovery. The obituaries all quoted from an interview Mr. Bennis had done with the *Harvard Business Review* in 2009: "The process of becoming a leader is similar, if not identical, to becoming a fully integrated human being."

When we lead ourselves to become all that we can be, we can then lead others. We do this purposefully through taking positions or informally through taking action. People will look to us, at the examples that we live, and perhaps choose to walk similar paths.

Being led willingly is a choice, too. It gives permission for another to provide direction because you believe in where they are going or what they stand for. Being led does not mean surrendering your responsibility to evolve. It is easier to follow another than to do the work to lead yourself. Being led willingly is a commitment to staying present, acting with intention, and keeping purpose front and center in your mind.

When you choose to lead yourself, you can provide others with the impetus, the courage, and the self-investment to lead themselves as well. And when people are leading themselves, evolving and accomplishing on the path to becoming "integrated human beings," there is much good that can be done.

So please take this ADVICE: choose to take control of how you respond to life, lead yourself, be an inspiration to others, and lift a glass to all you can do to continue to become.

Cheers.

Acknowledgments

CRAFTING THIS BOOK TOOK a very specific cocktail: two parts David, two parts Liz, and one part Robin.

Without the encouragement, propulsion, and brilliance of Robin Torres, the idea for this book might have never made it off a cocktail napkin. Her ADVICE is always invaluable. The elegant, unique, and delightful David Bell bought breakfast at the finest hotels while we talked about leadership. He read versions of this manuscript and introduced me to Atria. David Woolfe, a brilliant writer in his own right, helped me find my voice after decades of academia's silencing of it. Liz Woolfe, wife of David and my best friend since the ninth grade, the most literate person I know, and my most ardent cheerleader, is the only being to have read every iteration of this book. Liz Stein took me on before Atria accepted the book and helped me tell my story with patience and skill. Wonderful embellishments came from Leslie Meredith, who helped me become a better writer, and then Sarah Cantin, both of Atria, who proved that she loves "all of her children the same." My agent, Monika Verma, has the patience of a saint and managed this newbie with humor and grace. Judith Curr—thank you for giving me this chance with Atria.

To all the wonderful people in my California family, the Minnesota Circle, at Happy Buddha Yoga, and the "Dirty Girls," and to all who read the manuscript, encouraged me, fed me, walked me, laughed with me, and cried with me, I am grateful to have you in my life.

And to my four-legged and two-legged family, thanks for the love—Zoe for being a fan, and Alex for listening to my dreams in the bathtub.

About the Author

PROFESSOR HELEN N. ROTHBERG was a bartender in New York City during college and while completing her PhD in organizational and policy studies, collecting an MBA in organizational behavior and becoming a master of philosophy in behavioral science along the way. To this day, despite all those years in school, she claims that everything she knows about leadership and management she learned as a bartender. It was behind the bar that she learned the most valuable lessons—from the restaurant owner, the staff, and the customers. Since that time, she has consulted with Fortune 500 companies, small technology start-ups, and not-for-profit organizations. Helen began writing this book more than seven years ago. She speaks regularly on the subject of bartending and leadership at alumni and student gatherings as well as for associations and company special events such as "Better Than Chocolate" for Health Quest and the holiday gala for the Strategic Capabilities Network in Ontario. She is professor of strategy at the School of Management at Marist College and a senior faculty member at the Academy of Competitive Intelligence. With G. Scott

Erickson, she has published two books, twenty refereed articles, and ten book chapters on the intersection of intellectual capital and competitive intelligence. She lives in Orange County, New York, with her husband, dog, and two or three part-time goats, and she still mixes a mean cocktail.